A Glimpse of the Christian

More Glimpses of God's Grace

Richard J. "Dick" Hill

CROSSBOOKS
PUBLISHING

CrossBooks™
A Division of LifeWay
1663 Liberty Drive
Bloomington, IN 47403
www.crossbooks.com
Phone: 1-866-879-0502

First published by CrossBooks 05/01/2014

ISBN: 978-1-4627-3683-6 (sc)
ISBN: 978-1-4627-3682-9 (hc)
ISBN: 978-1-4627-3684-3 (e)

Printed in the United States of America.

This book is printed on acid-free paper.

CONTENTS

INTRODUCTION

A Glimpse of the Christian is a follow-up book to *A Glimpse of the Christ*, which features small insights into the identity and work of Jesus Christ. *A Glimpse of the Christian* emphasizes short glimpses into the identity and work of Christians.

I went to a pastors' meeting recently and overheard two brothers questioning their call to the ministry. Think of this! They were wondering aloud why in the world they did not pursue a different educational path that would have given them a career to fall back on. This caught my attention, and I settled in to listen more carefully. Both men were discouraged about the ministries that God had placed them in. They were not sufficiently motivated to stay the course amidst all the obstacles they were facing.

I consider God's call to preach His Word to the world as the highest calling a human being can have. However, some find it hard to remain faithful amid the many pitfalls in ministry–the money that does not come in to pay the bills, church leaders who feel obligated to take a stand against everything the pastor suggests, disgruntled church members who think it is necessary to keep something negative stirred up all the time–not to mention the personal family pressures. I wanted to say, "Fellows, don't you remember how and why the living God called you to himself in the first place?"

I thought back to my own reasons for hanging tough through the years. How had I been motivated to hang in there through it all? I am drawn back to the amazing glimpse of grace I received in 1989 during a morning walk. God used it to change the course of my entire ministry. I was going through a particularly rough time with the congregation I was leading; I was looking to God for answers and pondering some passages I had recently studied.

Centuries ago, Paul faced the same opposition in preaching the gospel that I was facing. He found that he had to defend himself before the very people who should have trusted him. I identified with that! Some even accused him of using the gospel to serve his own selfish desires. Quitting was never an option for Paul or for me. Paul said that we are hard pressed on every side, yet not crushed. We are perplexed but not in despair, persecuted but not forsaken, struck down but not destroyed.

What enabled Paul to persevere in the face of such suffering? He thought back to the day of his own dramatic Damascus Road conversion when he met Jesus Christ face to face. It has always been fascinating to me that God blinded Paul so that he could really *see* for the first time. From that day on, his ministry was to advance the cause of Jesus Christ rather than his own. He gave one of his famous conclusions marked by the word "therefore."

> Therefore we do not lose heart. Even though our outward man is perishing, yet the inward man is being renewed day by day. For our light affliction, which is but for a moment, is working for us a far more exceeding and eternal weight of glory, while we do not look at the things which are seen, but at the things which are not seen. For the things which are seen are temporary, but the things which are not seen are eternal. (2 Cor. 4:16-18)

I am painfully aware that my outward man is perishing. My body is growing older and wearing out. I do not have all the time in the world to finish the purpose that God has set me apart to do.

Paul went further. We are not to lose heart, because the spiritual man inside is being renewed day by day. This is a comforting thought. No matter what is going on around us, the Holy Spirit is constantly renewing our minds and is steadily conforming us to the image of Jesus Christ.

What an encouragement! But how is this possible? Paul made this amazing contrast. He said that our momentary light affliction is working for us a far more exceeding and eternal weight of glory. What exactly did Paul mean by *momentary light affliction*? He tipped his hand in the same book. Read the story of his life.

> In labors more abundant, in stripes above measure, in prisons more frequently, in deaths often. From the Jews five times I received forty stripes minus one. Three times I was beaten with rods; once I was stoned; three times I was shipwrecked; a night and a day I have been in the deep; in journeys often, in perils of waters, in perils of robbers, in perils of my own countrymen, in perils of the Gentiles, in perils in the city, in perils in the wilderness, in perils in the sea, in perils among false brethren; in weariness and toil, in sleeplessness often, in hunger and thirst, in fastings often, in cold and nakedness—besides the other things, what comes *upon* me daily: my deep concern for all the churches. (2 Cor. 11:23b-27)

Momentary light affliction! Up against that backdrop, my problem with the congregation didn't appear to be so bad. Paul said that all he was going through in this life paled in significance when compared to the eternal weight of glory that awaited him. Seeing Christ face to face far outweighed the effects of an aging body–the suffering, the defeats, all the heartaches in this life.

What Paul said next became the motivation for my life's ministry. He said that I was to begin looking beyond the things that human eyes can see and begin to peer into God's unseen world. The things that I see with my physical eyes are destined to pass into oblivion. They are just temporary, passing things. The things that I cannot see with my human eyes are eternal things.

God impressed upon me that I am to use the eyes in my mind to see the unseen. My thoughts went quickly to these words of Jesus Christ: "But blessed are your eyes for they see, and your ears for they hear." He was obviously not speaking of human eyes or human ears. My mind raced on to a third passage that I had recently studied. Contrasting human wisdom with God's wisdom, Paul wrote these incredible words that God etched forever into my mind.

> But as it is written: "Eye has not seen, nor ear heard nor have entered into the heart of man the things which God has prepared for those who love Him. But God has revealed them to us through His Spirit. For the Spirit searches all things, yes, the deep things of God. For what man knows the things of a man except the spirit of the man which is in him? Even so no one knows the things of God except the Spirit of God. Now we have received, not the spirit of the world, but the Spirit who is from God, that we might know the things that have been freely given to us by God. These things we also speak, not in words which man's wisdom teaches but which the Holy Spirit teaches, comparing spiritual things with spiritual. (1 Cor. 2:9-13)

God's wisdom is knowledge that cannot be seen with human eyes or heard with human ears. That sounded familiar. In fact, God's wisdom is that which has never entered into a human mind before. Incredible! That would mean that this wisdom is not the rehashed human understanding coming from the mind of man.

Paul then wrote something that has become the motivation for Glimpses of Grace Ministries and the day-by-day church ministries that God has led me to. He said that *God has revealed these hidden things to us through His Spirit.* Hold it! Is this saying what I think it is saying? Is Paul saying that God's Spirit opens to our human spirits the deep things of God, the hidden wisdom of God? Is he saying that we can know the things that human ears have never heard or eyes have ever seen? We can know the things that no human mind has ever thought. That is exactly what he is saying. This is fascinating!

How is this possible? The next line reads, "What man knows the things of a man except the spirit of the man, which is in him?" I alone know my own secret thoughts. Likewise, the Spirit of God alone knows the deep things of God. My mind began to race. We have received, not the spirit of this world, but the Spirit who is from God! *Why?* In order that we might know the things that have been freely given to us by God. The Spirit of God lives in me. He has a purpose for being there. He can teach me the deep things of God. We can know the things that have been freely given to us by God.

The final words of the passage "comparing spiritual things with spiritual" actually sent me into another world. The Holy Spirit brings to the mind spiritual thoughts as the words are read. As I study the written words of the Bible, verse by verse and line upon line, God the Holy Spirit opens the eyes of my mind to see and understand the deep, fascinating wisdom of God. That is absolutely incredible. We can know the mind of God!

Here's a catch. These glimpses into God's unseen world cannot be found by searching for them. God opens them to us at His pleasure as we study the Bible, word after word and line by line year after year. These glimpses are not unique to only one Christian. They are open to all. Since we have the Holy Spirit living in us, then we meet the criteria to receive them. And it is not different glimpses for different people. Every believer receives the very same truth.

God has not taught me everything that I have desired to know about His plan, but He has been pleased to give me small insights, small *glimpses*. These insights placed together began to etch a beautiful portrait in my mind. God has opened to me His incredible salvation plan, the true identity of Jesus Christ, the immense value of His death and resurrection, and the nature and purpose of the Holy Spirit, to name a few. These are glimpses of grace.

The Christian's relationship to Christ has everything to do with the invisible work of God the Holy Spirit. Christians become Christians by means of His work. Christians live their Christian lives also by means of the Holy Spirit. *A Glimpse of the Christian* features these ministries of the Holy Spirit:

- The Holy Spirit's work of regeneration (Titus 3:5)
- The Holy Spirit's work of baptizing (1 Cor. 12:13)
- The Holy Spirit's work of indwelling (1 Cor. 6:19-20)
- The Holy Spirit's work of equipping (1 Cor. 12:18)
- The Holy Spirit's work of sealing (Eph. 1:13-14)
- The Holy Spirit's work of teaching (Jn. 16:12-14)
- The Holy Spirit's work of controlling (Eph. 5:18)

Many books on the Christian life have as their theme what Christians are supposed to do. For example, Christians are people who busy themselves living moral lives, praying, preaching the gospel, going to church, studying the Bible, and attempting to make a godly impact on those around them.

All of this is true, but it is far more important to discover who we are as Christians. Why? Because *what* we do is based on *who* we are. We do not become Christians because we do Christian things. We are Christians; therefore, we do the things that Christians do.

So let's discover who Christians are and what Christians do.

CHAPTER 1

A GLIMPSE OF THE CHRISTIAN'S LIFE

The very first time the word *Christian* is found in the Bible is in the book of Acts. "And the disciples were first called Christians in Antioch" (Acts 11:26). King Agrippa said that Paul "almost persuaded him to become a Christian" (Acts 26:28), and Peter said, "If anyone suffers as a Christian, let him not be ashamed, but let him glorify God in this matter" (1 Pet. 4:16). That's it. Those three references are the only times in the Bible the word *Christian* is mentioned.

What does the word *Christian* mean? It means "belonging to Christ" or "connected to Christ." Some of the most exciting glimpses into God's invisible domain are the ones that teach us exactly how we are connected to Him.

True Christians know quite well that we are connected to Christ by faith and faith alone (Eph. 2:8-9; Rom. 4:4-5). Some folks erroneously believe that in order to be saved, human works must be added to faith. This is not the case. We receive God's gift of forever life by placing our faith alone in the person of Christ alone. However, the glimpses that I want us to see go far beyond our faith connection to Christ.

1

First and most importantly, Christians are Bible people. For most readers this would appear glaringly obvious. "Well, of course," you might respond, "what else would we be? The Bible is the source of the gospel and the source of our faith in Christ."

Then again, you may not understand exactly what I mean by *Bible people*. Christians believe the Bible to be God's inerrant, infallible word. We find the gospel of God's grace by which we are saved in the Bible. Christians are to be faithful to study the Bible, seeking to find the correct interpretation so we can do what it says and teach it accurately. But Christians are also people whose very existence is dependent on the Bible.

Let me explain!

THE BIBLE

There are books considered by many to be holy books: the *Hindu Veda*, the *teachings of Buddha*, the *Muslim Koran*, the *Book of Mormon*, and the Bible. People become Hindus because they are taught out of the *Veda*. Buddhists study and attempt to follow the teachings of Mahatma Buddha. Muslims believe and follow the teachings of the *Koran*. Mormons form their beliefs from both the Bible and the *Book of Mormon*.

However, there is no book equal to the Bible. There is only one God, and He has spoken. The apostle Peter said, "Knowing this first, that no prophecy of Scripture is of any private interpretation, for prophecy never came by the will of man, but holy men of God spoke as they were moved by the Holy Spirit" (2 Pet. 1:20-21).

The teaching contained in the Bible is not a record of man's thoughts about God. It is, in fact, God's word about himself.

How did God transfer His word from His mind to the pages of the Bible? The Holy Spirit moved special men to write down God's word as He dictated it to them. The writers' human wills were active, but the Holy Spirit was in complete control of everything they spoke and wrote. They used their own words, but every word was guided through the directing hand of God.

God used forty different writers to pen His word over a period of some 1600 years. The Old Testament was written in Hebrew, with a short portion written in Aramaic. The New Testament was written in Greek. The Bible has been translated from its original language into many languages, allowing God to speak to many nations and peoples around the world. From Genesis through Revelation, God's word–the Bible–is complete and completely truthful. God preserved and protected His word and brought it safely down to us today.

The result is that the Bible that we hold in our hands includes all the words with all their proper meanings that God intends for us to have. Every noun, verb, adjective, adverb, participle, infinitive, conjunction, and prepositional phrase is in the Bible by God's design. The Bible contains 1,189 chapters, 41,173 verses in the Old Testament, 33,214 verses in the New Testament, 593,393 words in the Old Testament, 181,253 words in the New Testament, and 774,646 total words.[1] The longest chapter is Psalm 119, and the shortest is Psalm 117. The longest book in the Old Testament is Psalms and the longest in the New Testament is Luke.

Let's ask the most searching question. Why did God choose to make His word known to us?

REGENERATION AND SEED

One does not have to be a Bible scholar or an expert theologian to understand how sinful people become Christians. All we need to know is a little something about the birds and the bees and the flowers and the trees, and we are there. God is the great genius. He penned the Bible for ordinary people who are acquainted with His creation. Arguably the most amazing and powerful glimpse into the invisible world of God is the Bible's teaching concerning *regeneration.*

The science of biological regeneration is a God-ordained fact of life. Following His initial creative act, God destined that all living organisms reproduce themselves. In the beginning, God established this unchanging blueprint.

> Then God said, "Let the earth bring forth grass, the
> herb that yields seed, and the fruit tree that yields fruit
> according to its kind, whose seed is in itself, on the earth;"
> and it was so. And the earth brought forth grass, the
> herb that yields seed according to its kind, and the tree that
> yields fruit, whose seed is in itself according to its kind.
> And God saw that it was good. (Gen. 1:11-12)

Thus God commanded what scientists call organic reproduction. It is what we refer to as the cycle of life. He created plants to grow and to produce seeds that regenerate other plants. He created trees that produce fruit containing seed, and the seed again regenerates the tree. Corn seeds regenerate corn plants and then corn, and the process starts again. Apple trees produce apples containing seeds, and the process starts again.

This reproductive cycle has held its pattern since the dawn of creation (Gen. 8:22). The seeds always produce fruit *after their kind.* James said that the fig tree does not produce olives nor does the grapevine produce figs (Jas. 3:12).

A seed can be stored away and lie dormant for years. It may give the appearance that there is no life within, but when it is placed into the ground, the whole of God's universe springs into action to cause germination. The earth turns on its axis, and the seasons change, bringing the spring.

The sun, which is located some 93,000,000 miles away, warms the soil to just the right temperature. The tides move in with the pull of the moon, causing the warm air to rise from the oceans and turn to tiny droplets of water. The wind currents move this moisture inland, producing condensation and the rain that waters the seed. The lightning flashes to produce the necessary nitrogen to fertilize the soil. The seed germinates, and another plant is born.

"God gives us rain from heaven and fruitful seasons, filling our hearts with food and gladness" (Acts 14:17). What an amazing thought! He is in absolute control of the whole process.

There are several documented records for the germination of old seeds. The most recent I found is dated June 2005. It was the seed of a date palm discovered during an archaeological excavation at King Herod's Palace on Mount Masada near the Dead Sea. The seed that produced this palm, nicknamed Methuselah, has been dated at approximately 2,000 years of age.[2]

My father-in-law has planted seeds in a vegetable garden for years. I have watched him prepare the soil by loosening the dirt and carefully mixing in the fertilizer along with a few of his secret recipes. He plants the seeds at just the right depth. From those seeds, I have enjoyed many good vegetables.

God also established a biological regeneration pattern for the animal world. He created sea creatures and birds and told them to *be fruitful and multiply on the earth.*

> And God said, "Let the waters abound with an abundance of living creatures…. Let the earth bring forth the living creature according to its kind: cattle and creeping thing and beast of the earth, each according to its kind"; and it was so. And God made the beast of the earth according to its kind, cattle according to its kind, and everything that creeps on the earth according to its kind. And God saw that it was good. (Gen. 1:20, 24-25)

The phrase *according to its kind* is repeated over and over. There are obvious genetic changes within the plant and animal world. There are different kinds of plants and different breeds of animals, but there is no crossing over from one species to another. Plants do not produce animals; animals do not produce plants; dogs do not produce cats; birds do not produce fish, and so forth. God's established order is in place.

CORRUPTED SEED

God created the first two human beings (Adam and Eve), and placed them in a beautiful garden called Eden. God told them to be fruitful and multiply and fill the earth (Gen. 1:26). He commanded them also to till the soil and to tend the garden (Gen. 2:15). It is reasonable to assume that the first couple learned about seeds and regeneration from their work in the garden. Through this garden God provided their every need. He told the couple to freely eat of every tree in the garden (Gen. 2:16).

There was one tree that Adam was forbidden to eat from, the tree of the knowledge of good and evil. God said that if they ate from that tree they would surely die (Gen. 2:17). This is the first time that death is mentioned in the Bible. Eventually the couple ate from the tree and immediately they died (Gen. 3:6). They did not fall over dead physically, yet they did die. How did they die? They died spiritually. When God created Adam, He gave him a body, soul, and a human spirit. The soul was that which connected Adam to the earth; it is earthy and natural.

The human spirit, on the other hand, is what connected Adam to God. The human spirit is what makes man different from animals. Before the fall, Adam and Eve were connected to God spiritually. They were created to know and fellowship with Him. When Adam sinned, his human spirit died. He became a natural man, separated from God.

After the fall, Adam and Eve began to reproduce in obedience to God's command (Gen. 4:1). True to God's formula, they reproduced *after their kind.* They were now sinners, and they began to reproduce a world of sinners.

> Therefore, just as through one man sin entered the world,
> and death through sin, and thus death spread to all men,
> because all sinned. (Rom. 5:12)

So death began to spread all over the world because Adam's physical seed had become corrupt, stained with death. He passed his death to all his children and to their children. The fallen couples' regenerated offspring were born to die.

As a part of the judgment for man's sin, God cursed the ground.

> "Cursed is the ground **for your sake**; In toil you shall eat
> of it all the days of your life. Both thorns and thistles it
> shall bring forth for you, and you shall eat the herb of the
> field. In the sweat of your face you shall eat bread till you
> return to the ground, for out of it you were taken; for dust
> you are, and to dust you shall return." (Gen. 3:17b-19)

It is strange that God said that the ground would be cursed for the sake of the fallen couple. Paul said that creation was subjected to futility, not willingly, but because of Him who subjected it in hope (Rom. 8:18). How can this curse of nature be a good thing? Built in this truth is the cycle of the seasons called in the Bible "seed time and harvest," the rotation of death and life. These cycles provide even today clear object lessons to every one of regeneration, seed germination, plants, plant growth and fruitful production. They are all connected, as we shall see, to an amazing truth contained in the Bible. This is remarkable and far more than mere coincidence.

HEAVENLY BIRTH

Let's plug into a familiar conversation between a very religious Pharisee, Nicodemus, and the Lord Jesus Christ. Nicodemus said, "We know that you are a teacher come from God because no one can do the miracles that you do unless God is with Him" (Jn. 3:2).

As we say in the South, "Our Lord cut right to the chase." Jesus said bluntly, "Most assuredly, I say to you, unless one is born again, he cannot see the kingdom of God" (Jn. 3:3). In fact, Jesus gave Nicodemus no option. He said, "You must be born again" (Jn. 3:7).

Nicodemus was obviously stunned! He responded, "What, can I enter a second time into my mother's womb and be born?" (Jn. 3:4). Physical birth was the only kind that he knew anything about.

Jesus responded, "Unless one is born of water and the Spirit he cannot see the kingdom of God." What did Jesus mean by being born of water and the Spirit? "Born of water" cannot mean literal water, for this would mean that a physical substance–water–could produce something spiritual by washing away sins. That cannot happen. H_2O cannot make the flesh spiritual! One cannot produce a spiritual birth through physical means.

Jesus was not bringing up water baptism, as many may assume. All the saints named in Hebrews 11 were declared right before God by faith. Salvation is not of works but by faith. Water baptism is a human work. Christ came to save, yet He did not baptize (Jn. 4:2).

If water baptism is necessary for eternal life, Paul should have kept good baptismal records, but he did not. He said:

> I thank God that I baptized none of you except Crispus and Gaius, lest anyone should say that I had baptized in my own name. Yes, I also baptized the household of Stephanas. Besides, I do not know whether I baptized any other. For Christ did not send me to baptize but to preach the gospel. (1 Cor. 1:14-17)

Paul was not demeaning water baptism, but he clearly kept it separate from the gospel. The ritual of water baptism is not a part of the gospel that saves us.

The new birth that Jesus spoke of is a spiritual birth, and it can only be produced by spiritual means. God's word has the power to make one clean, like water. Jesus told His disciples, "You are already clean because of the word which I have spoken to you" (Jn. 15:3).

Paul said that *Christians* are those who have been "washed clean by the word of God" (Eph. 5:26). Jesus mentioned the Spirit's use of His words to impart life when He said, "It is the Spirit who gives life; the flesh profits nothing. The words that I speak to you are spirit, and they are life" (Jn. 6:63). When one is born of water and the Spirit that means the person is born again when the Spirit of God uses the word of God to impart life. The word of God takes on a spiritual power to produce a cleansing.

This heavenly birth is understandably called a washing of *regeneration.*

> When the kindness and the love of God our Savior toward man appeared, not by works of righteousness which we have done, but according to His mercy He saved us, through the washing of regeneration and renewing of the Holy Spirit, whom He poured out on us abundantly through Jesus Christ our Savior, that having been justified by His grace we should become heirs according to the hope of eternal life. (Titus 3:4-7)

Since regeneration involves the planting and germination of seed and since God saves us by the amazing seed of His word, we are thus regenerated. We are saved not by our own works of righteousness but through *regeneration* and *renewing* of the Holy Spirit. The Holy Spirit makes it all happen.

Regeneration is a combination of the Greek words *palin* (another) and *genesia* (birth). *Regeneration* means "another birth." What a glimpse of God's grace!

Our Lord's overwhelming point to Nicodemus is that the natural person affected by the fall of Adam must be made a spiritual person in order to see the kingdom of God. Christians are physical people who are made spiritual people.

In order to live forever with God, one needs neither reformation nor religion. One does not need to follow the teachings of Islam or Buddha, or become a devout Hindu or a Mormon or a Jehovah's Witness, or even to follow the example and teachings of Jesus Christ. A person does not need to become a Baptist or a Presbyterian or a Catholic or an Episcopalian. One needs to be *born of God.* Christians are people who are connected to Christ by birth.

LIVING SEED

It is through the teaching of the new birth that the genius of God can be clearly seen. Incredibly, He allowed at least two kinds of seed to slip past the corruption of the fall. These two seeds become the very reason that we are connected to Christ. The first is the miracle seed of the woman, the conception and birth of the living word–the Lord Jesus Christ (Gen. 3:15; Jn. 1:1-3). Jesus Christ was conceived by the Holy Spirit (Lk. 1:35). He bypassed the corrupt seed of the Adamic race by being born of a virgin. He was born physically alive and spiritually alive. He came as the sinless Lamb of God in order to die for us.

The other seed that God allowed to remain alive is the living seed of the word of God. The writer of Hebrews said that the word of God is living and powerful (Heb. 4:12). This seed is being used by God to regenerate a new people, a heavenly people, called Christians.

The apostle Peter taught this miraculous truth. He was encouraging believers to obey the truth of the Bible, keep themselves clean before God, and to love the brethren. He focused on the one thing that made this possible–a new birth.

> Having been born again, not of corruptible seed but incorruptible, through the word of God which lives and abides forever, because "All flesh is as grass, and all the glory of man as the flower of the grass. The grass withers, and its flower falls away, But the word of the LORD endures forever." And this is the word which by the gospel was preached to you. (1 Pet. 1:23-25)

Remember Jesus had told Nicodemus, "You must be born again." Peter's words, "Having been born again," however, are past tense. Peter had obviously been born again. He assumed that his readers also had made the trip. This new birth is the reason that God gave us His word. This new birth truth explains who Christians are. When you think of it, it is an incredible glimpse into God's amazing plan.

If man truly died spiritually in Adam, and this death separated him from God, then God must make a new birth happen in order to reconnect the person with God. The words *born again* actually mean "born from above." This new birth is heavenly.

Peter was careful to make a serious contrast between seed that is corruptible and that which is incorruptible. It is not corruptible seed that produces this new birth. The fall made this impossible. Corruptible seed produces life that is destined to die–*after its kind.* God uses the imperishable seed of His word to germinate life that lasts forever–*after its kind.*

Peter quoted from Isaiah 40:6-8 to prove his point: "All flesh is as grass." All members of the human race are like grass. "And all the glory of man is like the flowers of the grass." With fallen man there is a passing glory. "But the grass withers and the flower fades, but the word of God endures forever." As the grass dries up and the flowers fade, so human beings wither, and the glory that is attached to us is soon past. Human life and human glory are temporary.

James said, "Life is like a vapor that appears for a little while and then it is gone" (Jas. 4:14). In contrast, Peter said that the word of God endures forever. Jesus said, "Heaven and earth shall pass away but my word shall never pass away" (Matt. 24:35). The life that this seed produces will never die.

Peter called the portion of the word that brings eternal life *the gospel.* "Now this is the word which by the gospel was preached to you." The gospel is the truth concerning the identity, the death, and the resurrection of the God-Man, the Lord Jesus Christ. The gospel is the theme of the Bible.

Admittedly, our association with Adam's sin and death is extremely bad news. But the bad news makes the gospel wonderful news beyond anything that our human minds can grasp. God gave the command that the wages of man's sin would be death. But He also determined that He was going to pay that debt. Yet God, as God, could not die. God is eternal life, and eternal life is eternal. In order to die, God became a member of the human race, which was the most amazing transformation in all of history. The first Christmas morning in Bethlehem of Judea, through the womb of the Virgin Mary, God slipped into the world. Jesus Christ is God manifest in human flesh (Col. 1:16).

Born without sin, Jesus Christ went to the cross and died to pay for our sin. Paul wrote, "God made Him who knew no sin to become sin for us that we might be made the righteousness of God in Him" (2 Cor. 5:21). This living seed is capable of giving life to the dead. The Holy Spirit guides this truth into the dead mind, and there He germinates the seed and spiritual life is conceived. This amazing conception makes the gospel the most important news on this planet.

James gave a brief glimpse of this same spiritual phenomenon. Speaking of God, he wrote, "Of His own will He brought us forth by the word of truth, that we might be a kind of first fruits of His creatures" (Jas. 1:18). "Of His own will" expresses God's personal decision. This phrase, grammatically speaking, is called a *genitive of source.* It is from the source of God's own choice that He brings us forth.

Brought us forth is one word in the original language (*apokueo*). It is a birthing term meaning "to beget," or "to give birth to." God is the One who gives this birth. Note carefully again what God uses to regenerate this birth. God births us by the word of truth, His amazing seed. As a result of this birth, fallen human beings become the "first fruit of His creatures." *First fruits* is speaking of a new beginning, a new generation of people unstained by the corruption of the fall. These people are called *Christians.*

POWERFUL SEED

The gospel, when guided by the Holy Spirit, is the only power on earth capable of infusing spiritual life into the spiritually dead. This is why Paul was "not ashamed of the gospel of Christ, for it is the power of God to salvation for everyone who believes, for the Jew first and also for the Greek" (Rom. 1:16).

It was in Bible College that I first began to witness the power of the gospel. The entire sophomore class went on a witnessing trip to the beach. The point of the outing was to share the gospel with as many people as would take time to listen to us. I was teamed with a small girl named Nelda Salee. She walked up to a stately looking, tanned fellow and began to share with him the facts that Christ died for sin and that He had been raised again. She asked him if he would believe in Christ.

That was when things became a little tense. He responded with a barrage of intellectual sounding words, denying everything she had said. He began to scientifically attack the credibility of the identity of Christ and His resurrection.

Her response was beautiful. She said, "I don't know about all that, but I do know that if you will believe in Christ you will have eternal life."

He came back with another round of attacks, attempting to discredit her. She replied, "I don't know about all that, but I do know that if you will trust Jesus Christ to save you, He will." This went back and forth for some time. I remember feeling the overwhelming urge to jump into the conversation, but God held me back.

I watched in amazement as something began to happen. This man grew quiet and stopped his verbal attack on Nelda. He calmed down, and right there on the sand, he gently fell to his knees and acknowledged that he wanted to accept Jesus Christ as his Savior. Why? The powerful seed of the gospel is the dynamite of God. Does this mean that everyone will respond positively to it? Not at all! The Spirit of God must make it happen. But the power of God is in the message not in the messenger.

The gospel is God's supernatural seed that the Holy Spirit plants into the soil of the mind, and when the Spirit germinates it, it results in faith in Christ and new life. It has the power to break through every barrier, every objection, every human argument, and all the rationalization that is thrown against it. The simplicity of the gospel insults both man's intelligence and his pride. No amount of education, success, or wealth can give us a spiritual birth. Only the gospel wielded by the Holy Spirit of God can make it happen.

The Bible alone contains God's divine seed that the Holy Spirit uses to conceive spiritual life in those who hear and believe.

HEAVENLY PEOPLE

Adam's fallen seed is in the process of producing a civilization "after his kind." It is a civilization of sinful people that are locked in time and space and, like grass, they are all destined to die and perish. Human glory and all that sheds light upon man–pride, wisdom, beauty, talent, wealth, achievement–are temporary, and fame is fleeting. It appears briefly like a vapor, and it is quickly gone (Jas. 4:14).

Jesus Christ, as the last Adam, is using the spiritual, incorruptible seed of the word of God to generate a heavenly people after its kind, destined to live forever. Though we now have bodies that reflect our great-grandfather, Adam the first, we are destined to have bodies like Jesus Christ's glorious resurrection body.

> For our citizenship is in heaven from which we also eagerly wait for the Savior, the Lord Jesus Christ, who will transform our lowly body that it may be conformed to His glorious body, according to the working by which He is able even to subdue all things to Himself. (Phil. 3:20-21)

Paul clearly described these new bodies. They will have a new glory that pleases God, they will be made of a new kind of flesh, and they will be powerful spiritual bodies that will not perish (1 Cor. 15:38-43).

The two Adams and the civilizations that they produce will reflect the nature of each of them. The first Adam produced a physical civilization made from the dust. Paul said, "It is written that the first man Adam became a living being" (1 Cor. 15:45).

The last Adam, the Lord Jesus Christ, is breathing the gospel into the minds of many, giving us spiritual life. "The last Adam became a life-giving spirit" (1 Cor. 15:45). Paul said that the spiritual is not first but the physical. Afterward comes the spiritual (1 Cor. 15:46).

Paul then made his contrast of the two Adams clear. The first Adam was a man of the earth, made of dust. The second man is the Lord from heaven, the Lord Jesus Christ (1 Cor. 15:47). Paul said, "As was the man of dust, so are those who are made of dust. And as is the heavenly Man, so are those who are heavenly." Note this amazing glimpse! "As we have borne the image of the man of dust, we shall also bear the image of the heavenly Man" (1 Cor. 15:49).

Jesus said it like this, "That which is born of flesh is flesh and that which is born of the Spirit is Spirit" (Jn. 3:7).

I remember as a little boy walking through fields and finding seeding dandelions. I would pull the plant and blow the tiny, fluffy, parachute-like seeds into the air and watch them float away. I discovered later that some could travel several miles from the parent plant before finding enough soil to germinate. I did not realize then that God was in charge of those wind currents and that He was aware of the destiny of every small seed.

In like manner, throughout the generations of human history, the Lord Jesus Christ has unleashed the seeds of His word into the world. God's Holy Spirit has guided these seeds, depositing them into the soil of human minds all over the earth. These tiny seeds may be read directly from the Bible, preached from a podium, read from a printed page, or even sung.

Sometimes the seeds lie dormant for many years, maybe wrapped in an old dust-laden Bible tucked away on some bookshelf or in a small crevice in a grass house hidden in a remote jungle. Or they may be lodged in the memory bank of someone's mind for years. God moves heaven and earth to get the seeds precisely where He wants them to be. When He is ready, the Holy Spirit germinates those seeds and a brand new life occurs.

Several years ago I had the opportunity to go to Vijayawada, India, to teach the Bible to Indian pastors. So where did all the local churches come from that were represented by all these pastors? I was told that Bibles written in the language of the people had been smuggled into India and distributed throughout the land. Those who had come to faith in Jesus Christ did so through reading and listening to the word of God. Churches sprang up and grew based solely on the ministry of God's living seed. What an amazing glimpse!

One of the recipients of God's word was considered to be the most dangerous man in all of India. His gang attacked, plundered, and terrified many of the villages of a certain area. He was wanted, dead or alive. While ransacking through a room in one of the houses in a village, he found a little black book. At first he started to throw it away, but he noticed that the pages were very thin, just the right thickness to roll his cigarettes.

Each evening after a meal, Ramad relaxed with a smoke. He would take out a page in the little book, fold it, and roll it around his tobacco. One evening while rolling up the paper, he noticed that the writing was in his own language. So each evening he read the words on the page before he rolled it to smoke.

One evening he knelt down and trusted Jesus Christ as his Savior. The small black book was the Bible. Ramad had been born again from the living seed of the word of God. He gave himself up to the authorities. They quickly tried him and sent him to prison. The prison became his personal mission field. The Holy Spirit had moved the amazing seed of the living word of God into that prison through this bandit turned prisoner of Christ.[3]

God's spiritual seed always accomplishes its divine purpose. Speaking through the prophet Isaiah around 700 B.C., God said:

> For My thoughts are not your thoughts, nor are your ways
> My ways, says the LORD. For as the heavens are higher
> than the earth, so are My ways higher than your ways, and
> My thoughts than your thoughts. (Isa. 55:8-9)

God's thoughts tower high above the thoughts of this fallen civilization. God does not think like us for one very simple reason. He is not like us! To our way of thinking, strength is strength, weakness is weakness, intelligence is intelligence, and foolishness is foolishness. But in God's mind, the strongest things are the weakest, and some of the seemingly weakest things are the strongest, and some of the wisest things are the most foolish.

God delights in turning human wisdom inside out and upside down. The world promotes great wealth, superior intelligence, extreme popularity, and high position. These are things that God places on the bottom.

> For as the rain comes down and the snow from heaven,
> and do not return there but water the earth and make it
> bring forth and bud, that it may give seed to the sower
> and bread to the eater. So shall My word be that goes forth
> from My mouth; It shall not return to Me void, but it shall
> accomplish what I please, and it shall prosper in the thing
> for which I sent it. (Isa. 55:10-11)

God sends the rain and snow down to the earth, and then He returns it to the sky as vapor, but it does not return until it accomplishes its purpose. It causes the earth to bring forth and bud that it may produce seed for the sower and bread for the eater. The water always accomplishes that which God ordains it to accomplish. Likewise, God's word always accomplishes that which pleases God.

God's word comes from Him, generation after generation throughout the centuries, and it does not return to Him without accomplishing its appointed task. It always finds its target. God does not arbitrarily cast the seed of His word into the winds, allowing it to fall where it will. Nor does He hope that someone by chance will stumble across it, hear it, and respond to it.

The Holy Spirit directs the spiritual seed to minds from every nation, kindred, and language group. Through the generations of man God determines both the path and the performance of His spiritual seed. If the gospel is faithfully preached for years and only a few trust in Jesus Christ as Savior during that time, then that is God's design. God's word will never return to Him without completing its heavenly mission. Jesus said, "He who is of God hears God's words" (Jn. 8:47a). Christians are connected to Jesus Christ by birth. What a glimpse!

Chapter 2

A Glimpse of the Christian's Position

Christians are connected to Christ not only by birth but also by baptism. I know what you may be thinking. Today, when the word *baptism* is mentioned, water automatically jumps into our minds. But *baptize* in the New Testament means "immersion for the purpose of identification." We should not assume that this immersion always involves water.

Meeting with His disciples, Jesus told them that He was going away and that they could not come where He was going. He promised that He would prepare a place and return to get them (Jn. 14:1-6). In the meantime, He gave these instructions:

> And I will pray the Father, and He will give you another Helper, that He may abide with you forever–the Spirit of truth, whom the world cannot receive, because it neither sees Him nor knows Him; but you know Him, for He dwells with you and will be in you. I will not leave you orphans; I will come to you. A little while longer and the world will see Me no more, but you will see Me. Because I live, you will live also. At that day you will

know that I am in My Father, and you in Me, and I in
you. (Jn. 14:16-20)

Jesus told the disciples that during His absence He would ask the
Father to send them a helper. This helper would be someone of the
same kind to come along side of them and help them. They may not
have realized it, but this helper had been *with them* all along. This
invisible support is God the Holy Spirit. The heart of this incredible
information is that the Spirit would eventually be *in them*. He called
this helper the Spirit of truth–the Holy Spirit.

The Spirit would be sent to them on a special day that Christ
marked out as *that day*. Notice the three spiritual transactions that
would take place on that day. Christ said that His disciples would
know (1) that He was in His Father, (2) that they would be in Him,
and (3) that He would be in them. This sets up an incredible glimpse
into God's spiritual world.

Let's determine first what our Lord meant by *I in my Father.*
Soon after speaking these words, Jesus Christ died on the cross as
a substitute for our sin (2 Cor. 5:21). He was buried and was raised
from the dead (Matt. 28:6). He appeared personally to many people
in His glorified body, confirming to them that He had, in fact, come
back bodily from the grave (1 Cor. 15:5-6). Jesus met one last time
with the disciples, telling them to not leave Jerusalem but to wait
there for the coming of the promised Spirit (Acts 1:4). After giving
parting instructions from Mount Olivet, He was lifted into the air,
departing planet earth (Acts 1:9). What a sight that must have been!

We can map perfectly the destination of Christ from the book
of Hebrews. He went into heaven and was seated upon the throne at
His Father's right hand (Heb. 10:12-13). It is from that vantage point
that He continues to build and direct His church (Eph. 4:14-16). He
is carrying out His role as our High Priest by continuously giving us
access to God's throne through prayer and making intercession for
us to the Father (Heb. 8:1-2).

The "I in my Father" part of His prophecy had then been fulfilled (Jn. 14:20). The "you in Me and I in you" parts were yet to come. The "you in Me" prophecy has everything to do with baptism.

The Bible's teaching on baptism is very important and extremely misunderstood. There are both *dry baptisms* and *wet baptisms* mentioned. The wet baptisms involve water; the dry baptisms do not. The fascinating truth is that the dry baptisms are real identifications, while the wet baptisms are symbolic identifications.

Both real and symbolic baptisms were illustrated in the ancient world. During Paul's day, real baptism was associated with dyeing cloth. If a person wanted to dye a garment a different color, he took it to the baptizer man. This "baptist" was not a preacher but one who operated a laundry. One could take a tunic to the laundry and have it immersed into a vat of dye. The identity of the tunic would be changed from one color to another. If the dye was purple, the tunic became purple. If the dye was red, the tunic became red.

The color of the cloth was changed, so the immersion could illustrate real immersion. Keep this illustration in mind as we continue to investigate Christian baptism.

Symbolic baptism was also performed in the ancient world. A Roman soldier went through a ceremony to commission a new weapon. He ceremonially dipped a new sword into a vat of pig's blood. This ritual symbolically identified the sword as an instrument for taking lives or the shedding of blood.[4] The sword was not really changed. This was a picture of symbolic immersion.

Wet Baptisms

Wet baptisms involve real H_2O, but the ritual itself is symbolic. It merely pictures real truth.

John's Baptism

Speaking of the Jews who were coming to him to be baptized in the Jordan River, John said: "I indeed baptize you with water unto repentance, but He who is coming after me is mightier than I, whose sandals I am not worthy to carry" (Matt. 3:11).

The Jews who were being baptized in water had believed John's message that the kingdom was at hand and that the King was in their midst. This immersion symbolized the invisible truth of their turning from the sin of rebellion against God and their belief that the kingdom was about to come. Water baptism publicly identified them as subjects of the kingdom. The baptism did not *make* them kingdom people; it *identified* them as such. The baptism was symbolic.

The Baptism of Christ

Jesus Christ was also immersed into water.

> Then Jesus came from Galilee to John at the Jordan to be baptized by him. And John tried to prevent Him, saying, "I need to be baptized by You, and are You coming to me?" But Jesus answered and said to him, "Permit it to be so now, for thus it is fitting for us to fulfill all righteousness." Then he allowed Him. When He had been baptized, Jesus came up immediately from the water; and behold, the heavens were opened to Him, and He saw the Spirit of God descending like a dove and alighting upon Him. And suddenly a voice came from heaven, saying, "This is My beloved Son, in whom I am well pleased." (Matt. 3:13-17)

John was right to question Jesus concerning His baptism. Jesus Christ had no sin. However, Jesus took on flesh to identify with a sinful human race. This is why He submitted to John's baptism. He said that His baptism would fulfill all righteousness.

The word *righteousness* is the Greek word *dikaiosune*. It means to be adjusted to the righteous standard of God. Jesus' baptism identified Him as the one who was to become sin for man. He identified himself with sinners.

Hundreds of years before Christ's coming, Isaiah had declared that the Messiah "was numbered with the transgressors; yet He

Himself bore the sin of many, and interceded for the transgressors" (Isa. 53:12).

Jesus first act of ministry was to be symbolically numbered with those whom He had come to save. The sinless Son of God submitted to a baptism that was associated with sinners. In this act the Savior of the world revealed that He came to be identified with the sinners of the world, yet He was not a sinner. His baptism created the public platform from which He could be identified as the people's Messiah.

Believer's Baptism

Believers in Jesus Christ are publicly recognized today as such by immersion into water (Matt. 28:19-20). Physical water cannot make a sinful heart clean; it cannot give one new birth. It is a symbol. It is a picture of an invisible truth. Christian water baptism identifies those who have been spiritually immersed into a permanent union with the body of Christ. The water represents the body of Christ. The immersion symbolizes being identified with His death and resurrection. It is a water immersion, but it reveals a spiritual immersion.

DRY BAPTISMS

In contrast to wet, real baptisms are dry. One of the dry baptisms has everything to do with our being a Christian. Confused? Read on!

The Baptism into Moses

> Moreover, brethren, I do not want you to be unaware that all our fathers were under the cloud, all passed through the sea, all were baptized into Moses in the cloud and in the sea. (1 Cor. 10:1-2)

Moses and the Jews followed God's cloud and fire as He led them out of Egypt. They came to the Red Sea. Standing before the water, they saw the dust of the Egyptian army approaching. God instructed

Moses to hold his rod out over the waters. The sea parted, and the Jews walked across on dry land (Ex. 14:13-16).

The people identified themselves with Moses, following him into the sea. They were baptized into Moses. Neither Moses nor the Jews got wet that day. The Egyptians, on the other hand, did; and they did not fare too well (Ex. 14:17-31).

The Baptism of Fire

The baptism of fire is when Jesus Christ will identify all unbelievers with fire. The baptism of fire is also a dry baptism. The Lord Jesus will one day immerse all who do not believe in Him into unquenchable fire. John the Baptist said that he baptized with water but that one was coming after him who would baptize with the Spirit and with fire (Matt. 3:11). John then explained this strange fire baptism. Speaking of Christ, he continued: "His winnowing fan is in His hand, and He will thoroughly clean out His threshing floor, and gather His wheat into the barn; but He will burn up the chaff with unquenchable fire" (Matt. 3:12).

Jesus Christ is going to literally baptize with fire those who reject Him. Paul described Christ's baptism of fire this way:

> And to give you who are troubled rest with us when the Lord Jesus is revealed from heaven with His mighty angels, in flaming fire taking vengeance on those who do not know God, and on those who do not obey the gospel of our Lord Jesus Christ. (2 Thess. 1:7-8)

The baptism of fire is going to be a horrible time for many, but the warning is clear.

The Baptism of the Spirit

Christ's "you in Me" prediction has everything to do with Spirit baptism. No Bible truth is more important for understanding the true identity of Christians than this one, yet few Bible teachings have been more distorted and unclear. Dr. Howard Hendricks said,

"When Satan blinds people to Bible truth, he always blinds in areas that are crucial, never trivial."[5] He always blurs those truths that are meant by God to lead us to Christ or the truths that help us to grow in faith.

Satan has attempted to distort the true identity of the Christ by attacking both His deity and His humanity. He has tried to smear the bodily resurrection of Christ. He has worked to blind people to the gospel by persuading men to add human works to the finished work of Christ. He has relentlessly attacked the credibility of the Bible. He also has done a masterful job of distorting the real meaning of the baptism of the Spirit.

There are those who teach that the baptism of the Spirit is a second work of grace, a second blessing that follows the initial salvation experience. They teach that this baptism gives Christians more "spiritual power." Others say that there are two Spirit baptisms. One is a baptism into the body of Christ; the other is the baptism into the realm of the Spirit. But these views are not correct.

The truth is this: Spirit baptism happens to every believer the moment he or she believes in Jesus Christ. Every Christian is literally identified with Christ. We are forever positioned in Him. This is absolutely miraculous!

Though unseen by human eyes, the very instant we believe in Christ we are removed from Adam the first and immersed into the last Adam, the Lord Jesus Christ. It is at that moment we become a part of His body. This is what Christ meant by His words, "you in Me."

I agree with David, "Such knowledge is too wonderful for me. It is high, I cannot attain it" (Ps. 139:6).

Mrs. Polson, my seventh grade English teacher, made us memorize the being verbs–am, is, are, was, were, be, being, been, have, has, had, do, does, did, shall, will, should, would, may, might, must, can, could. She emphasized the importance of these little words, and I am so glad she did.

Because of the meaning of the being verb *are,* the passage that reads, "Now you are the body of Christ" (1 Cor. 12:27) makes perfect sense to me. The Christian's being is that we *are* the body of Christ. We become a part of His body the moment we are baptized into Him.

How important is this truth? The church of Jesus Christ is built upon it. It is the very basis for our unity as Christians. "For by one Spirit were we all baptized into one body whether we be Jews or Greeks, bond or free; and have all been made to drink into one Spirit" (1 Cor. 12:13).

The sense of this verse could read, "For by means of one Spirit were we all baptized into one body." The Holy Spirit is the one baptizing, and the body of Christ is the target of the baptism.

Paul had asked, "Is Christ divided?" No, He is the head–the authority–of the body. Our head is at this time seated next to the Father in heaven, but His body is here scattered all over the earth. Is the head separate from the body? No! Is Christ proportioned out more to one group than to another? Hardly! The universal body of Christ is one unit. We are all placed into permanent union with Him.

Christ accomplished much while He was here bodily on the earth. Though He has now ascended into heaven, He is still accomplishing His ministry through His body.

Though we are gifted differently in the body of Christ and have different roles to play, we are all members of the body. It is ironic that there is a major division among Christians today over the very work that is designed by God to unite us.

That Day

When did this baptizing work of the Spirit begin? True to Christ's words, it began on that day (Jn. 14:20). "That day" we believe to be the Day of Pentecost. Let's recount the events of Pentecost. Prior to Christ's departure from earth, He gave some final instructions to His disciples. "He commanded them not to depart from Jerusalem, but to wait for the Promise of the Father, 'Which,' He said, 'you have heard from Me; for John truly baptized with water, but you shall be baptized with the Holy Spirit not many days from now'" (Acts 1:4b-5).

True to His words, the Father sent the Holy Spirit into the world. When the Spirit arrived, He began immediately to do exactly what our Lord said He would do. He began to baptize believers into Christ.

> When the Day of Pentecost had fully come, they were all with one accord in one place. And suddenly there came a sound from heaven, as of a rushing mighty wind, and it filled the whole house where they were sitting. Then there appeared to them divided tongues, as of fire, and one sat upon each of them. And they were all filled with the Holy Spirit and began to speak with other tongues, as the Spirit gave them utterance. And there were dwelling in Jerusalem Jews, devout men, from every nation under heaven. And when this sound occurred, the multitude came together, and were confused, because everyone heard them speak in his own language. Then they were all amazed and marveled, saying to one another, "Look, are not all these who speak Galileans? And how is it that we hear, each in our own language in which we were born? Parthians and Medes and Elamites, those dwelling in Mesopotamia, Judea and Cappadocia, Pontus and Asia, Phrygia and Pamphylia, Egypt and the parts of Libya adjoining Cyrene, visitors from Rome, both Jews and proselytes, Cretans and Arabs–we hear them speaking in our own tongues the wonderful works of God." So they were all amazed and perplexed, saying to one another, "Whatever could this mean?" (Acts 2:1-12)

One might observe that the phrase *filled with the Spirit* is found in this passage, but the word *baptism* is nowhere to be found. That is true, but baptism was occurring. How do we know? Peter later reported to a group of Jews the news that Gentiles were becoming a part of the body of Christ. Notice what he said after Pentecost.

> And as I began to speak, the Holy Spirit fell upon them, as upon us at the beginning. Then I remembered the word of the Lord, how He said, "John indeed baptized with water, but you shall be baptized with the Holy Spirit." (Acts 11:15-16)

Peter remembered that just before Pentecost Christ said that believers "would be baptized with the Spirit" (Acts 1:4-5). After Pentecost, Peter said that this baptism had begun. Although the word *baptize* is not found in Acts 2, Peter said that the Spirit's baptism had begun and was continuing to happen.

The Day of Pentecost was the start of a new phase of God's kingdom on earth. It marked the beginning of the formation of the church–the body of Jesus Christ.

All believers, on the Day of Pentecost, were both filled and baptized with the Holy Spirit. The Day of Pentecost was a special day on God's calendar and can never be repeated any more than the crucifixion and resurrection of Christ.

Today, centuries later, the moment we believe in Christ we experience the same phenomenon. We are supernaturally baptized with the Spirit into the body of Christ. This, along with regeneration, is what makes us Christians. Every Christian has been baptized into Christ.

John wrote, "And we know that the Son of God has come and has given us an understanding, that we may know Him who is true; and we are in Him who is true, in His Son Jesus Christ. This is the true God and eternal life" (1 Jn. 5:20).

This baptism is no longer accompanied with supernatural signs, nor is it marked by emotional outbursts. Spirit baptism happens regardless of how the believer feels.

The Bible identifies Christians in many ways. We are called the body of Christ (1 Cor. 12:27), the temple of God (1 Cor. 6:19-20), Christians (Acts 11:26), little children (1 Jn. 13:33), believers (Acts 5:14), the church (Acts 2:47), the elect (Rom. 8:33), sons of God (Gal. 3:26), Abraham's seed (Gal. 3:29), and the circumcision (Phil. 3:3). Paul's favorite way of referring to Christians is those who are "in Christ."

Unto the church of God which is at Corinth, to them that are sanctified in Christ Jesus, called to be saints, with all that in every place call upon the name of Jesus Christ, our Lord, both theirs and ours. (1 Cor. 1:2)

But of Him you are in Christ Jesus, who became for us wisdom from God–and righteousness and sanctification and redemption. (1 Cor. 1:30)

Now he who established us with you in Christ, and has anointed us, is God. (2 Cor. 1:2)

Paul, an apostle of Jesus Christ by the will of God, to the saints who are at Ephesus, and to the faithful in Christ Jesus. (Eph. 1:1)

Blessed be the God and Father of our Lord Jesus Christ, who has blessed us with all spiritual blessings in the heavenly places in Christ. (Eph. 1:3)

Paul and Timothy, the servants of Jesus Christ, to all the saints in Christ Jesus who are at Philippi, with the bishops and deacons. (Phil. 1:1)

To the saints and faithful brethren in Christ who are at Colossae: Grace be unto you, and peace, from God, our Father, and the Lord Jesus Christ. (Col. 1:2)

For you brethren, became followers of the churches of God which in Judaea are in Christ Jesus; for you also have suffered like things of your own countrymen, even as they have of the Jews. (1 Thess. 2:14)

What a fascinating glimpse of God's grace. The moment we are saved we are immersed into Christ, making known that the second part of Christ's amazing prophesy, "you in Me," is being fulfilled. Christians are those who are forever in Christ. It is little wonder that this became Paul's favorite way of identifying Christians.

Chapter 3

A Glimpse of the Christian's Transformation

I have always been fascinated with God's biological wonder of metamorphosis. The caterpillar crawls out onto a small branch, ties itself to the branch and spins itself within a cocoon. Over a period of time that worm is transformed into a beautiful butterfly. This is an accurate illustration of what happens to a sinner who is baptized into Jesus Christ. Paul penned this miraculous truth.

> If anyone is in Christ, he is a new creation; old things
> have passed away; behold, all things have become new.
> (2 Cor. 5:17)

The moment the Holy Spirit places us into Christ, we are instantly changed from being part of an old creation to becoming part of a new creation. Spiritually, we put on Christ–like a robe. Paul said that as many as are baptized into Christ have put on Christ (Gal. 3:27). Just as the color of cloth is changed when it is submerged into dye, those who are submerged into Christ are changed forever. New things come and old things go!

Old things does not refer to the old sins that plagued us in the past. The sin nature resides in our physical bodies. Paul wrote, "For I know that in me, that is in my flesh, nothing good dwells; for to will is present with me, but how to perform what is good I do not find" (Rom. 7:18). See also James 1:13-15, 4:1-2.

As long as we remain attached to this body of flesh, we will possess both the temptation and the capacity to sin. John wrote, "If we say that we have no sin, we make God a liar and the truth is not in us" (1 Jn. 1:8).

Old things is a reference to the characteristics that linked us with the old Adam. We are all born connected to him (1 Cor. 15:22; Rom. 5:12). We were all old Adamites, his image having been stamped upon us. When we receive Christ, the Holy Spirit takes us from the old Adam and moves us into the new Adam, the Lord Jesus Christ (1 Cor. 15:45). When we are joined to Him, His characteristics become ours.

- In the first Adam we are born with an old temporary human life. In the last Adam we receive His life, eternal life.
- In the first Adam we had an old righteousness that is condemned by God's law. In the last Adam we receive His righteousness written in on our account. It is a righteousness that meets the required standard of God's law.
- In the first Adam we had an old relationship connected to the realm of Satan as children of darkness. In the last Adam we received His relationship to the Father. He is the Son of God. Therefore, we become children of God.
- In the first Adam we had human distinctions that separated us from one another. In the last Adam we receive His Christ-likeness in which all these barriers are broken down.
- In the first Adam we were citizens of old planet earth. In the last Adam we received His citizenship as citizens of heaven.

- In the first Adam we were imprisoned in an old physical body that is ordained to die and to perish. In the last Adam we are destined to receive a new body just like the body that Christ has, designed by God to live forever.
- In the first Adam we were slaves to sin and fated to spend forever in a place called hell. In the last Adam we become Christ's servant kings destined to reign with Him in His heavenly kingdom.

OLD BIRTH, NEW BIRTH

As stated in chapter one, we were all born into this world through a physical, flesh-and-blood birth connected with old Adam. His physical death seed corrupted us. Every human being who is born of a human father is born physically alive but spiritually separated from God. That means each one of us is born into this world as a sinner. While in this state, the Bible calls us *natural* people (1 Cor. 2:14).

In order to know God, this dead human spirit must be made alive. This is what makes the new birth absolutely necessary. We must be made *spiritual* people (1 Cor. 2:15). "The first man Adam became a living being; the last Adam became a life-giving spirit" (1 Cor. 15:45).

God the Spirit directs the supernatural seed of the gospel into our dead human minds. The Spirit germinates that seed, and spiritual life is conceived. Faith is then placed in Jesus Christ and our dead human spirit is made alive. At that moment Christians are baptized into Christ. His life becomes our life. This all happens instantly. We are immediately transformed from spiritually bankrupt to spiritual billionaires.

Paul simply said, "He made us alive who were dead in trespasses and sins" (Eph. 2:1).

John wrote, "And this is the testimony: that God has given us eternal life, and this life is in His Son" (1 Jn. 5:11). Notice that John said that our life is found *in God's Son.* This is astounding unseen truth!

OLD RIGHTEOUSNESS, NEW RIGHTEOUSNESS

The Bible presents a God of perfect righteousness. Speaking of God, Moses wrote:

> He is the Rock, His work is perfect; for all His ways are justice, a God of truth and without injustice; righteous and upright is He. (Deut. 32:4)

The word *righteous* is from the Hebrew word *tsedekah.* When referring to God, the word means "totally right." It does not mean very good or even very, very good or even extremely good, or enormously good, or almost perfect. It means absolutely, one-hundred-percent perfect. God is the very essence of righteousness.

When we seek to discover what "right" really is, we must use the plumb line of God's character. The apostle John said, "God is light and in Him is no darkness at all" (1 Jn. 1:5).

In order to live with God forever, we must possess righteousness equal to His own. Why? God's required righteousness is the righteousness that His righteousness requires Him to require.[6] God cannot compromise His character, not one small bit. He cannot allow anyone into His heaven who does not meet His absolute standard (Rev. 21:27). His eyes are too holy to even look upon sin (Hab. 1:13).

The major problem facing all of us is that every human being of Adam's race was born into this world without the righteousness necessary for life with God. This is what it means to be a sinner. "For all have sinned and fall short of the glory of God" (Rom. 3:23).

The problem gets worse because there is nothing we can do to earn this righteousness. Nothing. We cannot earn it by stopping all our bad habits, reforming our lives, or turning over new leaves. We cannot earn it by being good, becoming religious, attending church, or by joining some religious group.

How do we know for sure that we have fallen short of God's required righteousness? Our righteousness is measured against the standard revealed by God's famous Ten Commandments. They are clear (Ex. 20:3-17).

- You shall have no other Gods before you.
- You shall not make for yourselves any graven image.
- You shall not take the Lord your God's name in vain.
- Honor your father and mother.
- Remember the Sabbath day to keep it holy.
- You shall not kill.
- You shall not commit adultery.
- You shall not steal.
- You shall not bear false witness against your neighbor.
- You shall not covet.

God requires that these commands be kept. In fact, in order for them to give us life, they must be kept perfectly our whole life. Jesus said that if one even thinks of committing adultery it is as though the act has been committed. To break just one brings a curse from God. "Cursed is everyone who does not continue in all things which are written in the book of the law to do them" (Gal. 3:10).

James said, "For whoever shall keep the whole law, and yet stumble in one point, he is guilty of all" (Jas. 2:10). If we break just one commandment–openly or mentally–then we are not right! This proves that we are sinners and that we have come short of God's glory.

These commands cannot be kept by faith. One must actually keep them and keep them all in order to be justified by them. "But that no one is justified by the law in the sight of God is evident, for 'the just shall live by faith.' Yet the law is not of faith, but 'the man who does them shall live by them'" (Gal. 3:11-12).

The Ten Commandments reveal and demand God's righteous requirement, but they cannot provide righteousness. If they could have made a person right before God, Christ should not have died. Note carefully Paul's words. "I do not set aside the grace of God; for if righteousness comes through the law, then Christ died in vain" (Gal. 2:21).

If keeping the Ten Commandments had given us the necessary righteousness for salvation, then righteousness would be made possible by keeping the law. But that was never God's plan. Paul wrote further: "For if there had been a law given which could have given life, truly righteousness would have been by the law" (Gal. 3:21).

Why did God give us the law? Paul's testimony gives us the reason.

> What shall we say then? Is the law sin? Certainly not! On the contrary, I would not have known sin except through the law. For I would not have known covetousness unless the law had said, "You shall not covet." But sin, taking opportunity by the commandment, produced in me all manner of evil desire. For apart from the law sin was dead. I was alive once without the law, but when the commandment came, sin revived and I died. And the commandment, which was to bring life, I found to bring death. For sin, taking occasion by the commandment, deceived me, and by it killed me. (Rom. 7:7-11)

Paul said clearly that the problem is not with God's law. God's law is not the sin. It is designed by God to *reveal* the sin, to make the sin known. Paul would not have known that he was a sinner before God until God the Holy Spirit unleashed the spirit of God's law in his heart. Paul recognized that he was a covetous person because God's holy law told him so. God's law tells everyone to be perfectly right according to these rules or die. Far from the potential of making us right before God, the law brings a curse (Gal. 3:10).

Paul called God's holy commandments *a ministry of death* and *a ministry of condemnation.*

> But if the ministry of death, written and engraved on stones, was glorious, so that the children of Israel could

not look steadily at the face of Moses because of the glory of his countenance, which glory was passing away, how will the ministry of the Spirit not be more glorious? For if the ministry of condemnation had glory, the ministry of righteousness exceeds much more in glory. (2 Cor. 3:7-9)

In order for us to know that we need a Savior, we must first realize that we are sinners. God's commandments bring this conviction of sin. The law tells us that we are sinners and must die. It tells us that we need a righteousness that we do not have. It is through this understanding of our sin that God reveals His grace.

God took on human flesh and came into this world as the sinless Son of God. Because Jesus Christ was born of a virgin, He missed Adam's sin (Matt. 1:23-25; Lk. 1:27-33). He lived a perfect life (Jn. 8:46), and the absolutely perfect Son of God died in our place. Christ took in His own body the condemnation that should have been ours.

Christ has redeemed us from the curse of the law, having become a curse for us (for it is written, "Cursed is everyone who hangs on a tree") that the blessing of Abraham might come upon the Gentiles in Christ Jesus, that we might receive the promise of the Spirit through faith. (Gal. 3:13-14)

In order to be right before God, we must be positioned in Jesus Christ. The wages of sin is death and every sinner must die, but it makes all the difference in the world where we die. All who are baptized into Christ become identified with His death (Rom. 6:3; Gal. 2:20). The death for sin that we owe to God is paid in Christ. Christians die in Him, and in Him we receive the righteousness that we need for life.

He made Him who knew no sin to become sin for us so that we might be made the righteousness of God in Him. (2 Cor. 5:21)

When we are positioned in Christ, His righteousness is put to our account.

> And be found in Him, not having my own righteousness, which is from the law, but that which is through faith in Christ, the righteousness which is of God by faith. (Phil. 3:9)

In Him we are perfectly and forever adjusted to the righteousness of God. This is arguably some of the most incredible news on this planet.

We all will be measured against God's righteousness! God has set apart a special future day in which He is going to judge the entire human race by His righteous standard. Paul wrote these words to the people at Athens, Greece.

> Truly, these times of ignorance God overlooked, but now commands all men everywhere to repent, because He has appointed a day on which He will judge the world in righteousness by the Man whom He has ordained. He has given assurance of this to all by raising Him from the dead. (Acts 17:30-31)

Those who are "in Christ" will have the necessary righteousness to live forever. Those who are not in Christ will perish!

OLD CITIZENSHIP, NEW CITIZENSHIP

A continuing part of the "old things, new things" is that our physical birth makes us citizens of planet earth. We are locked in a physical body that is held upon this old planet by gravity. We are limited by both time and space. We have souls that are earthly. We think, reason, feel, and choose in this earthly realm. John said, "He who comes from above is above all; he who is of the earth is earthly and speaks of the earth" (Jn. 3:31).

> For many walk, of whom I have told you often, and now tell you even weeping, that they are the enemies of the cross of Christ: whose end is destruction, whose god is their belly, and whose glory is in their shame–who set their mind on earthly things. (Phil. 3:19)

Adam the first gave us this earthly citizenship. Since Jesus Christ is from above, when we are placed into Him, we also become citizens of heaven. We receive a new citizenship. This new citizenship gives us passports to a coming new world. "For behold, I create new heavens and a new earth; and the former shall not be remembered or come to mind" (Isa. 65:17).

Peter said that we are to look for this new heaven and new earth. "Nevertheless we, according to His promise, look for new heavens and a new earth in which righteousness dwells" (2 Pet. 3:13).

Jesus Christ is the firstborn, the prototype of this new civilization. "For whom He foreknew, He also predestined to be conformed to the image of His Son, that He might be the firstborn among many brethren" (Rom. 8:29).

Christ has become the progenitor of a new race of people. It is His ministry to bring many sons to glory. "For it was fitting for Him, for whom are all things and by whom are all things, in bringing many sons to glory, to make the captain of their salvation perfect through sufferings" (Heb. 2:10).

Christians become citizens of heaven.

> For our citizenship is in heaven, from which also we eagerly wait for a Savior, the Lord Jesus Christ; who will transform the body of our humble state into conformity with the body of His glory, by the exertion of the power that He has even to subject all things to Himself. (Phil. 3:20-21)

While on this earth, our identification cards could read "pilgrims and strangers here." We are just a passin' through! Speaking of those who were faithful in Hebrews 11, the writer of Hebrews concluded:

> These all died in faith, not having received the promises, but having seen them afar off were assured of them, embraced them and confessed that they were strangers and pilgrims on the earth. For those who say such things declare plainly that they seek a homeland. (Heb. 11:13-14)

Peter agreed with these words:

> Beloved, I beg you as sojourners and pilgrims, abstain from fleshly lusts which war against the soul. (1 Pet. 2:11)

Because we are now citizens of heaven, our names are already recorded there (Jn. 18:36).

> To the general assembly and church of the firstborn who are registered in heaven, to God the Judge of all, to the spirits of just men made perfect. (Heb. 12:23)

> And I urge you also, true companion, help these women who labored with me in the gospel, with Clement also, and the rest of my fellow workers, whose names are in the book of life. (Phil. 4:3)

The One who stamped our passports is already there. He has gone on ahead, promising to prepare a place for us that where He is we shall be also (Acts 1:11; Jn. 14:1-3). All of our spiritual relatives who have gone before us are there. Our inheritance has been shipped on ahead and is there (1 Pet. 1:4; Matt. 5:12; 6:20). We who have the life of God within us are under the rule of our heavenly High Priest while we are on this earth (Heb. 4:14-16), but someday heaven will be our home.

A missionary was returning home to America after a life spent sharing the gospel on another continent. The only transportation he could afford was on an old freighter. As they were steaming into the harbor, New York was welcoming a very important foreign dignitary to America. The bands were playing and fireworks were lighting up the night sky. The Statue of Liberty was in the background, and the confetti was flying.

Out in the darkness, the freighter steamed by with the old missionary leaning against the chains on the deck. There would be only a few from the mission waiting for him, and yet he had been involved in the most important work on this planet. *Why, Lord?* he thought. *I have served you my whole life and there is no one here to greet me.*

A sweet peace overwhelmed Him as he imagined the Lord saying, "Yes, but you're not home yet, son! Not yet!"

Christians are converted from an old citizenship to a new citizenship.

OLD RELATIONSHIP, NEW RELATIONSHIP

Another part our old connection to Adam the first is that we come into this world related to a fallen world ruled by the devil (Jn. 12:31). We are all born under his dominion as children of darkness.

Jesus said that we "once lived in darkness" (Jn. 12:46). Paul wrote this same truth when he said "you were once in darkness" (Eph. 5:8). He also said that "we have been delivered from the power of darkness" (Col. 1:13).

When Adam and Eve sinned, God pronounced a judgment against Satan for his part in deceiving man. God said to Satan in the garden, "And I will put enmity between you (Satan) and the woman, and between your seed (your offspring) and her Seed (her offspring). He shall bruise your head, (Jesus is going to kill Satan) and you shall bruise His heel" (Gen. 3:15).

Enmity is a word meaning "hostility." God told Satan that He would put opposition between Satan's offspring and the woman's seed. The woman's seed is a reference to Jesus Christ. Satan's offspring refers to all people related to him. It was a part of this crowd that crucified Jesus Christ (bruised his heel).

The offspring of Adam and Eve began with Cain and Abel. Cain was clearly marked out as being of the evil one.

> Not as Cain, who was of the evil one and slew his brother.
> And for what reason did he slay him? Because his deeds
> were evil, and his brother's were righteous. (1 Jn. 3:11)

Jesus Christ, in contrast, called Abel "righteous" (Matt. 23:35;
Heb. 11:4).

Many today remain under the dominion of Satan. Jesus, speaking
to a crowd of religious Pharisees, spoke these powerful words:

> You are of your father the devil, and the desires of
> your father you want to do. He was a murderer from
> the beginning, and does not stand in the truth, because
> there is no truth in him. When he speaks a lie, he speaks
> from his own resources, for he is a liar and the father of
> it. (Jn. 8:44)

Satan is busy blinding the minds of those who are trapped in his
domain, even religious leaders of the day.

> But even if our gospel is veiled, it is veiled to those who
> are perishing, whose minds the god of this age has blinded,
> who do not believe, lest the light of the gospel of the glory
> of Christ, who is the image of God, should shine on them.
> (2 Cor. 4:3-4)

The word *blinded* means giving them a sadistic anesthesia that
blinds their minds to the gospel. What is Satan's major means of
blinding people? Religion! He uses religion to tell people that they
can be good to get to heaven. He convinces people that there is a
spark of good in us and if we will just feed the flame we will make
it. Millions are blinded by this lie!

Why would they care to listen to the gospel? The gospel tells us
that we are not good. We are sinners and in need of a savior. People
who are satisfied in their religion are not looking for a way out.
Unless God removes the blindness, Satan will not allow the spiritual
seeds of the gospel to penetrate their thinking.

But God is opening the spiritual eyes of many, turning them from the dominion of Satan to God.

> In which you once walked according to the course of this world, according to the prince of the power of the air, the spirit who now works in the sons of disobedience, among whom also we all once conducted ourselves in the lusts of our flesh, fulfilling the desires of the flesh and of the mind, and were by nature children of wrath, just as the others. (Eph. 2:2-3)

Darkness must be turned to light. Jesus Christ is called "the life and the light of men" (Jn. 1:3-4). When we are positioned in Christ, we become connected to His life and light. As new creations, we pass from the darkness of the dominion of Satan into the kingdom of the Son. We become children of the living God.

> But as many as received Him, to them He gave the right to become children of God, to those who believe in His name. (Jn. 1:12)

> The Spirit Himself bears witness with our spirit that we are children of God. (Rom. 8:16)

> Beloved, now we are children of God; and it has not yet been revealed what we shall be, but we know that when He is revealed, we shall be like Him, for we shall see Him as He is. (1 Jn. 3:2)

Children of Satan must become children of God. This can only be accomplished by the preaching the gospel.

> To open their eyes so that they may turn from darkness to light and from the dominion of Satan to God, that they may receive forgiveness of sins and an inheritance among those who have been sanctified by faith in Me. (Acts 26:18)

> For you are all sons of God through faith in Christ Jesus.
> For as many of you as were baptized into Christ have put
> on Christ. There is neither Jew nor Greek, there is neither
> slave nor free, there is neither male nor female; for you are
> all one in Christ Jesus. (Gal. 3:26-27)

Jesus Christ is the very Son of God. The moment that we are baptized into Christ, we put Him on as we would put on a garment. This is another way of saying that we assume His identity. Like Him, we become the sons of God.

OLD DISTINCTION, NEW UNITY

Before Christ, there were racial, religious, cultural, and social barriers that separated us. We were born into this world separated by gender, age, and educational and social status. When we are placed into union with Christ, we lose all of these human distinctions.

> For in Christ Jesus neither circumcision nor uncircumcision
> avails anything, but a new creation. (Gal. 6:15)

For Christians, race is no longer an issue, nor are the other distinguishing characteristics mentioned above. We are all in Christ, and Christ is in us.

> Do not lie to one another, since you laid aside the old self
> with its evil practices, and have put on the new self who is
> being renewed to a true knowledge according to the image
> of the One who created him—a renewal in which there is
> no distinction between Greek and Jew, circumcised and
> uncircumcised, barbarian, Scythian, slave and freeman,
> but Christ is all, and in all. (Col. 3:10-11, NASV)

Before Christ is in us, these barriers may seem insurmountable. Racial and religious barriers separated the Greek and Jew, one circumcised and the other uncircumcised. They had nothing to do with each other. Jewish people refused to enter a Gentile house. They would not eat a meal cooked by Gentiles nor buy meat prepared by Gentile butchers. When they returned to Israel, they showed their scorn for Gentiles by shaking off the Gentile dust from their clothes and sandals. Even the apostles were reluctant to accept Gentiles as equal partners in the church (Acts 10-11). But the gospel broke down those barriers, and Jew and Gentile became one in Christ.

Paul described this new distinction to the church at Ephesus.

> But now in Christ Jesus you who once were far off have been brought near by the blood of Christ. For He Himself is our peace, who has made both one, and has broken down the middle wall of separation, having abolished in His flesh the enmity, that is, the law of commandments contained in ordinances, so as to create in Himself one new man from the two, thus making peace, and that He might reconcile them both to God in one body through the cross, thereby putting to death the enmity. (Eph. 2:13-16)

In Christ, all became equal partners in a spiritual relationship. Christians are brothers and sisters in Christ. There is no place for man-made barriers in the church since Christ is all and in all. Because Christ indwells all believers, all are equal (Gal. 3:26-28).

OLD BODY, NEW BODY

Another characteristic that indicates that we are tied to the old Adam is that we are born into this fallen world locked in a physically fallen body. This physical body is fashioned by God for this world. We are, as the Psalmist wrote, "wonderfully made" (Ps. 139:14). However, we begin to physically die the moment that we are born. Man's days are numbered; God alone determines them.

> Since his days are determined, the number of his months is with You; You have appointed his limits, so that he cannot pass. (Job 14:5)

> Man who is born of woman is of few days and full of trouble. He comes forth like a flower and fades away; He flees like a shadow and does not continue. (Job 14:1-2)

> All go to one place: all are from the dust, and all return to dust. (Eccl. 3:20)

> The days of our lives are seventy years; and if by reason of strength they are eighty years, yet their boast is only labor and sorrow; for it is soon cut off, and we fly away. (Ps. 90:10)

Our days in this fallen body are limited and our body will eventually begin to wear out. Ultimately, we all grow old, get sick, and die.

Those who have become new creations in Christ are promised brand new bodies. They will be magnificent bodies designed by God to live forever.

> For we know that if our earthly house, this tent, is destroyed, we have a building from God, a house not made with hands, eternal in the heavenlies. (2 Cor. 5:1)

God calls the old physical body an earthly house, a tent. A tent is a temporary dwelling. But one day this tent is going to be removed. We are going to die. When this happens, our address immediately changes. We move into a new body that God has prepared for us.

Paul described this heavenly body by answering questions about the resurrection like this, "How are the dead raised up, and with what kind of body do they come?" (1 Cor. 15:35).

Planted seeds have to die before they bring forth the life that is within them. Paul continued, "Foolish one, what you plant is not made alive unless it dies" (1 Cor. 15:36).

Paul described the new body using easy-to-understand illustrations from the plant world. He said that the plant that comes from the seed is far superior to the seed (1 Cor. 15:37). Flowers are far more beautiful than the seeds from which they come. The new body that God gives to believers is far superior to the old one.

Each new body will be unique (1 Cor. 15:38). The old saying that there is nobody on earth exactly like you is true. This will also be true with our new bodies. As God designed for us a physical body suited for this earth, He has also designed for each of us a body suited for eternity.

> All flesh is not the same flesh, but there is one kind of flesh of men, another flesh of animals, another of fish, and another of birds. (1 Cor. 15:39)

The new body will not have the flesh of men or of animals or of fish or of birds. God designed a flesh for each of these. Likewise, He is going to design a unique flesh for our new bodies.

> There are also celestial bodies and terrestrial bodies; but the glory of the celestial is one, and the glory of the terrestrial is another. There is one glory of the sun, another glory of the moon, and another glory of the stars; for one star differs from another star in glory. (1 Cor. 15:40-41)

The sun and moon and the heavenly bodies, like the stars, all differ from one another, each possessing its own beauty. Our new bodies also will be unique, each having its own glory.

Paul contrasted the old physical body that is buried with the new body that shall be.

> It is sown (buried) a perishable body but raised imperishable so also is the resurrection of the dead. The body is sown in corruption (death and decay), it is raised in incorruption (never to die or decay any more). It is sown in dishonor, it is raised in glory. (1 Cor. 15:42-43a)

At a Christian's funeral, the old body is placed back into the earth from which it was made. The new body is raised to glorify the creative genius of God. This is where we get the term "a glorified body."

Just as Adam produced human bodies that are destined to die and to perish, the Lord Jesus Christ, the last Adam, is producing a generation that will never die.

> There is a natural body, and there is a spiritual body. And so it is written, "The first man Adam became a living being." The last Adam became a life-giving spirit. However, the spiritual is not first, but the natural, and afterward the spiritual. The first man was of the earth, made of dust; the second Man is the Lord from heaven. As was the man of dust, so also are those who are made of dust; and as is the heavenly Man, so also are those who are heavenly. And as we have borne the image of the man of dust, we shall also bear the image of the heavenly Man. (1 Cor. 15:43b-49)

At the time of the resurrection, those who have died in Christ will be raised with this new body, or it may be given to believers who are alive at the time of the translation of the church into the heavens (1 Thess. 4:13-17; 1 Cor. 15:51-55).

Old Destiny, New Destiny

The second coming of the Lord Jesus Christ is the climax of history. Christ is now seated at the right hand of the Father's heavenly throne serving as the faithful High Priest for His people. He will one day return to earth in full glory, and He will not be going back alone. The redeemed of all the ages will be returning with Him.

> For it was fitting for Him, for whom are all things and by whom are all things, in bringing many sons to glory, to make the captain of their salvation perfect through sufferings. (Heb. 2:10)

All Christians were once on their way to an eternity separated from God. They were destined for a place called hell. Paul penned these ominous words:

> And to give you who are troubled rest with us when the Lord Jesus is revealed from heaven with His mighty angels, in flaming fire taking vengeance on those who do not know God, and on those who do not obey the gospel of our Lord Jesus Christ. These shall be punished with everlasting destruction from the presence of the Lord and from the glory of His power, when He comes, in that Day, to be glorified in His saints and to be admired among all those who believe, because our testimony among you was believed. (2 Thess. 1:7-10)

This *flaming fire* is a picture of the Lord Jesus Christ returning to earth in judgment of those who do not know Him (Jn. 3:18, 36). Fire is used in the Bible to represent God's judgment. Because God is absolutely righteous and absolutely just, He must always adjust that which is not right to His righteous standard. To do less would make Him less than God. Although hell was not created for man, God will use it to adjust all those who have rejected Him to His righteousness.

> The wicked shall be turned into hell, and all the nations that forget God. (Ps. 9:17)

> Let death seize them; Let them go down alive into hell, for wickedness is in their dwellings and among them. (Ps. 55:15)

Jesus was rebuking a group of Pharisees when He said, "Serpents, brood of vipers! How can you escape the condemnation of hell?" (Matt. 23:33).

Jesus also said, "And do not fear those who kill the body but cannot kill the soul. But rather fear Him who is able to destroy both soul and body in hell" (Matt. 10:28).

In the last days Satan himself will be cast into hell. All who have rejected Christ will spend eternity there.

> Then I saw a great white throne and Him who sat on it, from whose face the earth and the heaven fled away. And there was found no place for them. And I saw the dead, small and great, standing before God, and books were opened. And another book was opened, which is the Book of Life. And the dead were judged according to their works, by the things which were written in the books. The sea gave up the dead who were in it, and Death and Hades delivered up the dead who were in them. And they were judged, each one according to his works. Then Death and Hades were cast into the lake of fire. This is the second death. And anyone not found written in the Book of Life was cast into the lake of fire. (Rev. 20:11-15)

That is enough of the bad news! In Christ we receive a new destiny! There is much talk among Christians about heaven, where every child of God will eventually go (Rev. 21-22). But before we arrive in heaven, we have an earthly kingdom to go through. We are destined to reign with Christ in His kingdom on this earth.

> And I saw thrones, and they sat on them, and judgment was committed to them. Then I saw the souls of those who had been beheaded for their witness to Jesus and for the word of God, who had not worshiped the beast or his image, and had not received his mark on their foreheads or on their hands. And they lived and reigned with Christ for a thousand years. But the rest of the dead did not live again until the thousand years were finished. This is the first resurrection. Blessed and holy is he who has part in the first resurrection. Over such the second death has no power, but they shall be priests of God and of Christ, and shall reign with Him a thousand years. (Rev. 20:4-6)

All who have been placed into Christ have been converted from death to life, from an old righteousness to a new righteousness, from an old relationship to a new one, from being citizens of planet earth to being citizens of heaven, from an old distinction to a new unity, from living in an old, fallen, earthly body to the promise of a new body, and from an old destiny to a new destiny.

We have been transformed from an old creation into a new one. Once we have been born again, we will never again be the same. As we grow more to understand our new identity, hopefully "the things of earth will grow strangely dim in the light of His glory and grace."

CHAPTER 4

A GLIMPSE OF THE CHRISTIAN'S POSSESSION

Christians, as we have learned, are connected to Jesus Christ by a new birth and by a new position. We have also learned that Christians are people who have been transformed from an old life to a new life. Now we will see that we are also connected to Jesus Christ by a miraculous possession.

Recall once again the remarkable prophetic words of Christ found in John 14:20: "At that day you will know that I am in my father and you in me and I in you." Let's focus on the last part of the prophecy, "I in you." Jesus meant that there would come a time when He would personally dwell in His disciples. This promise was fulfilled on the Day of Pentecost. On that day the church of Jesus Christ was born.

There are great family traditions in the South, and church is one of the greatest of all. Heard in thousands of homes every Sunday morning is the question, "Hey, you goin' to church today?" Church may be a huge brick or concrete building in a large city or a simple wood-frame building in the country. It may be identified as Baptist or Methodist or Presbyterian or Pentecostal, to name a few, on a sign out front.

Church is where preaching and singing is heard, and, at times, where one is inspired, convicted, and even converted. Church is where families watch children grow up, get baptized, and marry. It is where friends and family meet and eat and talk about life. It is a momentary reprieve from the stresses of the world.

The kind of church one attends or what religious denomination one is part of likely depends on one's upbringing. Most seem to prefer a church with an air-conditioned and heated building, a steeple, organized meetings, Sunday School classes, great music, and dynamic age appropriate programs.

This brings up an interesting question: is the true church of Jesus Christ a building? The fact is, according to the Bible, it is a building. However, it is not a building made of brick, wood, or steel. Nothing could be further from the truth. Catch this glimpse! The church is a building *made of people.*

The word *church* in the original language is formed from two Greek words. The little preposition *ek* means "from" or "out from." The word *kaleo* means "to call." When put together, the word *ekklesia* means "to call out from." The church is made up of people whom God has called out from the world to be His very own possession. The church is God's people.

The God revealed in the Bible is infinite. This means that He goes far beyond our human ability to understand. We cannot begin to wrap our thoughts around Him. This entire universe with its countless billions of galaxies cannot contain Him. He exists outside of that which He created. That is an incredible thought!

Stephen made this point clear in his testimony before the Jews. He recalled the fact that Solomon built God a temple.

> However, the Most High does not dwell in temples made
> with hands, as the prophet said: "Heaven is My throne, and
> earth is My footstool. What house will you build for Me?
> says the LORD, or what is the place of My rest? Has My
> hand not made all these things?" (Acts 7:48-50)

GOD'S OLD ADDRESS

It is true that there was a time when God made himself known to the Jews by revealing His presence with a cloud and fire in a temple made with hands. This temple was to be a very special place. God handpicked craftsmen to build it. Each of these builders was adequately equipped and given special wisdom and talent. There were engineers, carpenters, brick masons, and other specialists. Moses wrote concerning them, "All who are gifted artisans among you shall come and make all that the Lord has commanded" (Ex. 35:10; 36:1).

They were told to follow an exact blueprint that God gave to Moses on Mount Sinai. "According to all that I show you, that is, the pattern of the tabernacle and the pattern of all its furnishings, just so you shall make it" (Ex. 25:9).

God made it abundantly clear why such great care was taken on the old physical earthly temple. He was to manifest His glory in that temple.

> Then the cloud covered the tabernacle *(temple)* of meeting and the glory of the Lord filled the tabernacle. (Ex. 40:34; see 1 Kings 6-8)

That must have been an incredible sight. People stood in awe and watched as the cloud and fire came down and rested upon the temple. The God who created them, the God who created this entire universe, visibly revealed himself to fallen human beings.

His presence made known in this way is called "the glory of the Lord" or, as some call it, the *shechinah glory.* In the Old Testament these manifestations of God were in the form of the angel of the Lord, light, fire, or a cloud, or a combination of these.

God continued to manifest His presence to Israel in the temple for many years, but the Jews began to rebel against Him. Their rebellion became so horrible that Ezekiel wrote that God's presence eventually left the temple. This extremely sad scene is described in

Ezekiel. God is shown as leaving in stages, each one showing His reluctance to go.

He first went from the mercy seat and paused over the threshold of the temple.

> Then the glory of the LORD went up from the cherub, and paused over the threshold of the temple; and the house was filled with the cloud, and the court was full of the brightness of the LORD's glory. (Ezek. 10:4)

From the threshold of the temple, He moved above and beyond the temple and stood at the eastern gate.

> Then the glory of the LORD departed from the threshold of the temple and stood over the cherubim. And the cherubim lifted their wings and mounted up from the earth in my sight. When they went out, the wheels were beside them; and they stood at the door of the east gate of the LORD's house, and the glory of the God of Israel was above them. (Ezek. 10:18-19)

Next the glory of the Lord went up from the east side of the temple and stood on the mountain.

> So the cherubim lifted up their wings, with the wheels beside them, and the glory of the God of Israel was high above them. And the glory of the LORD went up from the midst of the city and stood on the mountain, which is on the east side of the city. (Ezek. 10:22-23)

At last the word *Icabod,* which means "for the glory of the Lord has departed," was etched over the temple. What a horrible day that must have been!

GOD'S NEW ADDRESS

Hundreds of years passed. Then one day something amazing happened. Catch this glimpse! God moved into a new temple, a temple not made of wood or stone or bricks. A temple not filled with pews or laden with carpets or with windows filled with stained glass or beautiful rooms with hanging chandeliers. Fifty days after the resurrection of Jesus Christ, God sent the Holy Spirit, who located His presence within the bodies of all believers.

> When the Day of Pentecost had fully come, they were all with one accord in one place. And suddenly there came a sound from heaven, as of a rushing mighty wind, and it filled the whole house where they were sitting. Then there appeared to them divided tongues, as of fire, and one sat upon each of them. And they were all filled with the Holy Spirit and began to speak with other tongues, as the Spirit gave them utterance. (Acts 2:1-4)

The church of Jesus Christ–Christians from every nation, kindred and tongue–became the dwelling place of God that day. Speaking of Corinthian Christians, Paul wrote:

> Or do you not know that your body is the temple of the Holy Spirit who is in you, whom you have from God, and you are not your own? For you were bought at a price; therefore glorify God in your body and in your spirit, which are God's. (1 Cor. 6:19-20)

Paul later wrote:

> For you are the temple of the living God. As God has said: "I will dwell in them and walk among them. I will be their God, and they shall be My people." (2 Cor. 6:16)

Paul's letter to the church at Rome makes clear the same truth.

> Now hope does not disappoint, because the love of God has been poured out in our hearts by the Holy Spirit who was given to us. (Rom. 5:5)

The moment we become a Christian, God the Holy Spirit comes into our bodies and takes up permanent residence. In fact, the Spirit's presence is the absolute proof that we are connected to Jesus Christ.

> But you are not in the flesh but in the Spirit, if indeed the Spirit of God dwells in you. Now if anyone does not have the Spirit of Christ, he is not His. (Rom. 8:9)

Paul called the Holy Spirit "the Spirit of Christ." This is one of the miraculous things about the Trinity. The members of the Trinity are coexistent. When one member is present, all three are there.

> To whom God would make known what is the riches of the glory of this mystery among the Gentiles, which is Christ in you, the hope of glory. (Col. 1:27)

Paul expressed this same truth to the church at Galatia.

> I have been crucified with Christ; and it is no longer I who live, but Christ lives in me; and the life which I now live in the flesh I live by faith in the Son of God, who loved me and gave Himself up for me. (Gal. 2:20)

Finally, all of Christ's prophetic words in Jn. 14:20 were fulfilled. Christ is now in His Father, and we (Christians) are in Him, and He is in us! What an incredible thought! What an amazing glimpse into the unseen realm of a Holy God.

God's Living Temple

The church, therefore, is not a building made of physical material. It has never been. It is a spiritual house. Peter said:

> Coming to Him as to a living stone, rejected indeed by men, but chosen by God and precious, you also, as living stones, are being built up a spiritual house, a holy

> priesthood, to offer up spiritual sacrifices acceptable to
> God through Jesus Christ. (1 Pet. 2:4-5)

This is truth that no human eye has seen or ear heard. This is truth that has never before entered the mind of man. This is God's invisible reality revealed. Luke said:

> And on that day a great persecution began against the church in Jerusalem, and they were all scattered throughout the regions of Judea and Samaria, except the apostles" (Acts 8:1).

The church spread throughout all of Judea and Samaria. This is obviously not speaking of believers rushing out, busily drawing up blueprints and putting up physical buildings in these regions with communion tables, podiums, and stained glass windows.

Before Paul's conversion to Christ, this was said of him: "But Saul began ravaging the church, entering house after house, and dragging off men and women, he would put them in prison" (Acts 8:3). Saul persecuted the church, but it is extremely evident that he was not taking vengeance on a physical building. He was entering the houses in which the church met and persecuting people.

Before Saul changed his name to Paul, he became the most feared enemy of the church of Jesus Christ. He attempted single-handedly to destroy this new movement. It is interesting that when the Lord Jesus Christ called Saul of Tarsus to himself, He asked him a stabbing question: "Why are you persecuting Me?" (Acts 9:4).

Was Paul persecuting the body of Jesus Christ directly? Yes, he was! He was attempting to destroy believers and believers *are the body of Christ.*

Ask yourself as you read the following passages if the word *church* is speaking of a physical building or of people.

> Husbands, love your wives, just as Christ also loved the church and gave Himself up for her that He might present

to Himself the church in all her glory, having no spot or wrinkle or any such thing; but that she would be holy and blameless. For no one ever hated his own flesh, but nourishes and cherishes it, just as Christ also does the church, This mystery is great; but I am speaking with reference to Christ and the church. (Eph. 5:25-32)

So the church throughout all Judea and Galilee and Samaria enjoyed peace, being built up; and going on in the fear of the Lord and in the comfort of the Holy Spirit, it continued to increase. (Acts 9:31)

The news about them reached the ears of the church at Jerusalem, and they sent Barnabas off to Antioch. (Acts 11:22)

And when he had found him, he brought him to Antioch. And for an entire year they met with the church and taught considerable numbers; and the disciples were first called Christians in Antioch. (Acts 11:26)

Now about that time Herod the king laid hands on some who belonged to the church in order to mistreat them. (Acts 12:1)

So Peter was kept in the prison, but prayer for him was being made fervently by the church to God. (Acts 12:5)

Jesus Christ did not give himself on the cross for a physical building made of brick and mortar with stained-glass windows. Physical buildings do not enjoy peace. They do not hear. Steeples and stained glass do not pray. All of the following passages speak of the church as the living temple of God, not a building: Acts 13:1; Acts 14:23; Acts 14:27; Acts 15:3-4; Acts 15:22; Acts 18:22; Acts 20:17; Acts 20:28; Rom. 16:1; Rom. 16:5; Rom. 16:23; 1 Cor. 1:2; 1 Cor. 4:17; 1 Cor. 5:15; 1 Cor. 6:4; 1 Cor. 10:31; 1 Cor. 11:18; 1 Cor. 11:22; 1 Cor. 12:28; 1 Cor. 14:12; 1 Cor. 14:19; 1 Cor. 14:23; 1 Cor. 14:28; 1 Cor.

14:35; 1 Cor. 15:9; 1 Cor. 16:19; 2 Cor. 1:1; Gal. 1:13; Eph. 1:22; Eph. 3:10; Eph. 3:21; Phil. 1:2; Phil. 3:6; Phil. 4:15; Col. 1:18 Col. 1:24-25; Col. 4:15; Col. 4:16; 1 Thess. 1:1; 2 Thess. 1:1; 1 Tim. 3:5; 1 Tim. 3:15; 1 Tim. 5:16; Heb. 12:23; Jas. 5:14; 3 Jn. 1:6; 3 Jn. 1:9-10; Rev. 2:1; Rev. 2:8; Rev. 2:12; Rev. 2:18; Rev. 3:1; Rev. 3:7; Rev. 3:14

How did we ever get so far from this?

THE CHURCH BUILDERS

These words of Jesus Christ have become very important to us:

> And I also say to you that you are Peter and on this rock
> I will build My church, and the gates of Hades shall not
> prevail against it. (Matt. 16:18)

Jesus Christ entered this world through Bethlehem of Judea that first Christmas morning to become the king of the Jews (Lk. 1:32). Eventually He presented himself to them as such. However, after considering his miraculous credentials, these same people rejected Him and helped to crucify Him. Christ rose from the dead and postponed his earthly kingdom and returned to heaven.

All of these events did not catch God by surprise. This was all part of His plan. This plan is that Christ's literal, earthly kingdom will eventually come but that in the meantime He will build His church. His church–the operation of the body of Christ in this world– is a spiritual form of that kingdom now. God, what a genius you are!

The church in the New Testament is born again children of the living God called out from every nation, kindred, and tongue, whose purpose is to share the gospel and equip each other to serve God (Eph. 4:1-16). No place in the Bible do I find that unbelievers are encouraged to go to church. The Bible is filled with passages that command Christians to go into the world where non-Christians live and preach the gospel to them (Matt. 28:19-20; Acts 1:8; 1 Thess. 2:4).

One writer said, "Christians are not told to clean up the fishpond; we are told to fish in it." Another strong preacher of the past wrote,

"The Bible never tells the church to fight sin." We are told to "preach the gospel" (1 Cor. 9:27). The Holy Spirit will use only the power of the gospel to transform a life from sinner to saint, from the natural man to the spiritual man.

Jesus Christ did not leave His body on this earth to prepare us for heaven. We were just as prepared for heaven one second after we placed our faith in the Lord Jesus Christ as we will ever be. We are left here to carry the message of the gospel to the lost.

The number of local assemblies that are immersed in strong Bible study and serious worship continues to decline. In an attempt to make the gospel relevant, local churches are moving toward a market-driven mentality. The motto for church growth for many has become, "Do whatever is necessary to fill the place with people." Some Christian leaders say, "We are in competition with the world," and in order to compete we must get with the program. But the Bible says that we live "in the world but we are not of this world." We cannot compete with the world's system and ever hope to accomplish God's purposes. God will not allow us to do this.

The church is made up of people who have been born again by the amazing spiritual seed of the gospel, are baptized into Christ, are transformed, and have become the dwelling place of the Holy Spirit.

BUILDING THE CHURCH

Just as God selected and equipped gifted craftsmen to build the old physical temple, Jesus Christ has selected and equipped gifted craftsmen to build His new spiritual temple (Eph. 4:11). When Christ ascended back into heaven, He began this process.

> But to each one of us grace was given according to the measure of Christ's gift. Therefore He says: "When He ascended on high, He led captivity captive, and gave gifts to men." (Now this, "He ascended"—what does it mean but that He also first descended into the lower parts of the earth? He who descended is also the One who ascended

far above all the heavens, that He might fill all things.)
(Eph. 4:7-10)

THE APOSTLES AND PROPHETS

And He Himself gave some to be apostles, some prophets,
some evangelists, and some pastors and teachers. (Eph. 4:11)

Apostles and New Testament prophets were the first
communicators of the gospel of the death and resurrection of Jesus
Christ to the world. An *apostle* was one sent with a message. During
His short time on this earth, Christ poured His life into His disciples.
A *disciple* is a learner. Following Christ's resurrection, these learners
became Christ's apostles.

The church is built upon the foundation of the apostles and
prophets, Jesus Christ himself being the chief cornerstone.
(Eph. 2:20)

CONFIRMATION GIFTS

During the early years of the church, there were many deceivers
claiming to be apostles and prophets of God. They distorted the
message of God and attempted to deceive.

For such are false apostles, deceitful workers, transforming
themselves into apostles of Christ. (2 Cor. 11:13; see 2
Pet. 2:1)

These false teachers were not easily spotted. The imposters
looked and sounded pretty much like the genuine teachers. How were
the people God wanted to reach to know the difference? God gave
His apostles and prophets special miracle-working power to verify
their identity and the importance of their message.

How shall we escape if we neglect so great a salvation,
which at the first began to be spoken by the Lord, and

was confirmed to us by those who heard Him, God also
bearing them witness with signs and wonders and various
miracles, and gifts of the Holy Spirit, according to his own
will. (Heb. 2:3-4)

The signs of a true apostle were performed among you
with all perseverance, by signs and wonders and miracles.
(2 Cor. 12:12)

Signs were impressive miracles that no doubt shocked and
amazed those who witnessed them. They verified the identity of the
real apostles. The miraculous signs were meant to say, "Hey, listen!
I am who I claim to be and what I am about to say is indeed the very
word of God. Pay close attention!"

Prophets passed from the scene when the need for them no longer
existed. The Bible was compiled and completed and contains all the
word of God. It is no longer to be added to or taken from.

Until the day of His return to establish His promised Kingdom,
He will continue to build His church.

CHAPTER 5

A GLIMPSE OF THE CHRISTIAN'S GIFTEDNESS

As the living, spiritual organism of the church began to grow, a new group of workers came on the scene (1 Cor. 3:9-15; Eph. 4:7-16). These workers could be compared to carpenters, plumbers, electricians, and brick masons in a construction business. These gifted craftsmen are continuing up to this very day to build on the prepared foundation.

There are workers with the gift of *faith* (1 Cor. 12:9). These believers are equipped by God to trust Him to do what He said He would do. They have the desire to know and act upon the word of God regardless of the odds against them. Other believers observe the ministry of these gifted Christians and also learn how to live by faith.

The gift of *teaching* (Rom. 12:7) has at least two characteristics. This gift includes those who have a passion and ability to study the depth of the word of God and those who have the capacity to communicate its meaning to others. New believers have the opportunity to grow in grace and knowledge of the truth because of the ministry of these gifted believers.

Helps (1 Cor. 12:28) is the gift of serving the body of Christ behind the scenes. The person with this gift makes an excellent deacon. Serving unselfishly is often tedious and thankless.

The gift of *administration* (1 Cor. 12:28) is the ability to organize the local church ministry. Those with this gift are God's efficiency experts. They have a desire that God's work be carried out decently and in order (2 Cor. 14:40). They go about their business with such love and reverence for the Lord that they are a blessing to everyone.

The gift of *exhortation* (Rom. 12:8) is the gift of encouraging. The word literally means "to call to one's side." This is a great complementary gift to teaching. The teacher brings one to the point of saying, "I see that." The encourager brings that same person to the point of believing, "I can do that."

Those with the gift of *giving* (Rom. 12:8) are able to give to the Lord's work consistently, liberally, and cheerfully. They do so with such grace and obvious unselfishness that the church is built up by it. The giving is done without any secret reluctance or false pretense. It is not reserved for the wealthy only.

The gift of *mercy* (Rom. 12:8), so necessary and yet so misunderstood, is literally the ability to show mercy to the undeserving. Mercy is not justice. Justice is to give one what is deserved. Mercy is to give what is not deserved. Expectations are not placed on those who receive mercy from those with this gift. If the recipients deserved acts of mercy shown them, it would not be mercy.

Those with the gift of *evangelism* (Eph. 4:11) have the ability to present the gospel of God's grace with extreme clarity to anyone, anywhere, at any time. They also have an overwhelming desire to do so.

The gift of *shepherding* (Eph. 4:11) is the ability to guide, feed, and guard the church of Jesus Christ. The motivation that drives all of these gifted people is the conscious awareness that they are serving not merely the church, but its head, the Lord Jesus Christ.

Jesus Christ is continuing to build His "living temple" today. When the last member of this body is in place, our head–the Lord Jesus Christ–will return and remove His church from this planet (1 Thess. 4:16-17).

THE GIFT OF MIRACLES

Many have been given the false impression that the Bible is a book filled with one miracle after another. This is not true. Miracles, even in the Bible, are the exception rather than the rule. They occurred in small clusters as God unfolded His plan for man. They were always used to gain favorable attention to something important that the living God was doing.

There are three major outbreaks of miracles in the Bible. They are found surrounding the lives of Moses and Joshua, Elijah and Elisha, and the Lord Jesus Christ.

God used miracles to deliver Moses and the people of Israel from Egypt (Ex. 7-12). The rod became a snake; the river became blood; and there were the plagues of frogs, lice, flies, disease, hail, locusts, darkness, and finally the death angel. Through miracles, God convinced an unbelieving Egyptian pharaoh that Moses was His messenger and that the Israelites must be released.

During the times of the prophets Elijah and Elisha, Baal worship threatened Israel's relationship with the true God. Baal's false prophets attempted to convince the Jews that they were the true prophets. On Mt. Carmel, the living God and the false god Baal were pitted against one another in battle. Elijah graphically illustrated to the Jews that their God is God.

Elijah built an altar and asked the prophets of Baal to cry out to their god to light the fire of the altar. They did so from morning until night. They even cut themselves with knives to show their sincerity, but no fire came down. Elijah had the servants pour water on the altar three different times to make it more of a powerful illustration. He then asked God to light the fire. Fire immediately came down and consumed the wood, the water, and even licked up the dirt. God used this miracle to reassure the Jews that He is the living God and Elijah was His prophet (2 Kings 18:18-38).

Miracles surround another pivotal time in God's plan for the world. God became a man in the person of Jesus Christ and presented himself to Israel as their King. The Christ made His identity extremely clear by performing many incredible miracles. He demonstrated power over nature, disease, demons, and death itself.

Following Christ's death and ascension, He began His church. This new body was made up of both Jews and Gentiles. This was remarkable because for centuries God had worked exclusively through the Jews. Gentiles had been on the outside looking in. That was about to change abruptly.

It would take strong persuasion for the Jews to believe that God was really going to include the Gentiles in His plan. The Gentiles needed to be shown that they were indeed now accepted by the living God. They had spent their lives under the evil power of the elaborate ceremonies of the false fertility gods and goddesses. Those false religions had become a part of their culture.

A most amazing miracle was that God, for the first time in history, actually dwelled in the bodies of believers–both Jews and Gentiles. This began on the Day of Pentecost. It was, therefore, no surprise that miracles were present on that day. Does God continue to work miracles today? Yes. He reserves that right because He is God, but He works miracles at His discretion, not ours.

THE GIFT OF TONGUES

Recall once again that Jesus Christ had ascended back to the Father as He promised. He had earlier instructed the disciples to go to an upper room and wait for the baptizing work of the Holy Spirit. That is where His disciples met and waited (Acts 1:4-5). The Day of Pentecost came and, true to custom, Jews came from all over the world to Jerusalem to celebrate the festival. There were

Parthians, Medes, Elamites, Mesopotamians, Judeans, and people from Cappadocia, Pontus, Asia, Phrygia, Libya, and from as far away as Rome. These were Jews who had left the homeland to find work elsewhere.

Suddenly a noise was heard like a rushing mighty wind. There was no wind, just the noise, and the noise filled the place. This was a miracle that could be heard. And there appeared to them tongues as of fire resting on each one of them. This was a miracle that could be seen. All were filled with the Holy Spirit and began to speak with other tongues, as the Spirit caused them to speak.

All the people there heard and understood the speakers speaking in their own language "the wonderful works of God" (Acts 2:11). What did they hear? It is my opinion that along with other wonderful works was the gospel, the good news of the death and resurrection of Jesus Christ. These were Jews, but they were foreigners. They spoke Gentile languages. They were amazed that the ones speaking the language were Jews-Galileans. And they could not understand why they heard them speak in their own native tongue. They were all amazed and wondered what it meant. Some said, "Oh the Galileans are just drunk" (Acts 2:1-13). They were not drunk at all. What was happening was all in God's plan.

It was not by chance that Christ died precisely on the Jewish feast day of the Passover. After all, He was the Passover Lamb (1 Cor. 8:5). It was no coincidence that Christ was resurrected during the festival of the First Fruits, because His resurrection was the *first fruits* of a large resurrection to follow (1 Cor. 15:20).

It was not happenstance that Christ began His church on the Day of Pentecost. *Pentecost* means "fifty days." Pentecost happened exactly fifty days after Christ's resurrection.

For years the Jews had celebrated the festival of Pentecost by baking two different grains into one loaf of bread (Lev. 23:15-17). They really did not understand why God had instructed them to do that. Now they had the capacity to understand. Exactly fifty days after the resurrection of Christ, the Holy Spirit began placing both Jew and Gentile into the body of Christ, making them one body.

Two things became immediately apparent. First, God was temporarily setting aside Israel as a nation. The Jews had rejected the Messiah that God had sent them. They had helped to crucify Him. Because of this, they were under the discipline of God. Judgment was imminent.

Secondly, a new creation was being formed, the body of Christ (1 Cor. 12:13). This was a momentous time. It was accompanied with miraculous signs and wonders. The Jews always sought a sign (1 Cor. 1:22). A sound of a mighty wind was heard and the fire was seen.

The sounds and the sights were meant to say, "Hey listen, the Lord is starting His church. Pay close attention!"

WHAT WERE THE LANGUAGES?

There was something very unusual about the languages spoken on that day. Though they were real languages, the people speaking them had not learned them. God was causing the speaker to speak. That was the miracle! The word "unknown" in the King James Version was added by the translators and is not in the original. In fact, this has confused many people. The languages used were *known languages* commonly spoken all over the world. This is verified by the fact that each one heard others speaking in their own *dialekto,* or "dialect" (Acts 2:8). This Greek word is always used in connection with known languages. Later at Corinth the word *interpretation* is used (1 Cor. 14:13). It is used only with the interpretation of known languages.

WHY THE SIGN?

Pentecost was the beginning of the body of Christ. It was being built by hearing and believing the gospel of the death and resurrection of Christ. The importance was not the supernatural languages themselves but what the languages were communicating, the gospel.

The Holy Spirit was empowering these believers to preach the gospel. Paul gave us a tremendous clue as to the reason God chose to use the gift of languages on this particular day.

> Brethren, do not be children in understanding; however, in malice be babes, but in understanding be mature. In the law it is written: "With men of other tongues and other lips I will speak to this people; and yet, for all that, they will not hear Me," says the Lord. Therefore tongues are for a sign, not to those who believe but to unbelievers; but prophesying is not for unbelievers but for those who believe. (1 Cor. 14:20-21)

Paul quoted the prophet Isaiah, and his words take us back to a time when Israel, as a nation, was in rebellion against God. God had sent Isaiah to give Israel His message, which was that they should turn back to God or God would send the Assyrians to discipline them.

Isaiah gave them this message clearly and more than once. The people responded like this: "Who do you think we are that you should speak to us like babies? You give us precept upon precept, line upon line, here a little there a little. We understand what you are saying."

They understood, but they did not heed the warning. They missed it! Isaiah told them they would clearly know that they were under God's judgment when they heard the foreign speech in their homeland. The Assyrians would be in their land burning their homes and destroying their families. They would hear these foreigners speak to them with their "strange tongues." This *tongue* was the Assyrian language that would hurt their ears and remind them that God's judgment had come.

"Indeed, He will speak to this people through stammering lips and a foreign tongue" (Isa. 28:11). That is exactly what happened in Acts 2. The Jews as a nation were again in rebellion against God. They had rejected the Messiah and helped to crucify Him.

Catch this glimpse! God reached back and gave the same sign to them that He had used in the days of Isaiah. Tongues were a sign to unbelieving Jews that they were *once again* under His judgment and that God was changing His program. This time God used the Romans rather than the Assyrians. Titus Vespacian, the Roman general, was poised to take Jerusalem and destroy the temple.

God is the great genius! He never disciplines His children without giving them a way out. His way out for Israel on that day was to repent and turn to Jesus Christ as their Savior. This sign also illustrated that He was now going to include all nations represented by many different languages in His body. This is why fifteen countries are mentioned on the Day of Pentecost.

Unbelieving Jews were in Jerusalem that day from many provinces. They heard the gospel in their own languages–Gentile languages (Acts 2:5-8).

Tongues Ceased

The judgment to which the sign of the gift of tongues pointed came to pass. Titus destroyed both the temple and the city of Jerusalem in 70 A.D. There is ample evidence that the true Biblical gift of tongues ceased around 70 A.D. Both history and the Bible make this clear. Tongues were mentioned only in the earliest books of the New Testament.

First Corinthians was one of Paul's earliest letters (56-58 A.D.). When he wrote about tongues to the church at Corinth, he was not encouraging them to use tongues. It was to correct them for misunderstanding the nature and purpose of the gift and for misusing it.

Paul wrote at least twelve other books and never mentioned tongues again. He wrote much about the nature and purpose of spiritual gifts in two of his later books, Romans and Ephesians, but he did not mention tongues (Rom. 12:3-6; Eph. 4:11-16).

Peter never mentioned tongues. James never mentioned tongues. John did not mention tongues, nor did Jude. Jesus Christ never mentioned the gift of tongues. Tongues appeared only briefly in Acts and 1 Corinthians. Once the judgment of God came upon Israel, and once the body of Christ began, the signs that had accompanied its beginning ceased.

Chapter 6

A Glimpse of the Christian's Security

Is it possible for a Christian to lose his or her salvation? Does the Christian truly have eternal life? Or do we receive probationary life from God until we commit a sin serious enough to lose it? It should be obvious to the most casual Bible student that if eternal life can be lost, it was never eternal life.

> Jude, a bondservant of Jesus Christ, and brother of James,
> to those who are called, sanctified by God the Father, and
> preserved in Jesus Christ. (Jude 1)

One of the most cherished teachings in the Bible is the story of Noah and the great flood. God judged and destroyed the entire civilization of man, sparing only one family. The simple reason given for sparing Noah and his family was because Noah found grace in God's eyes (Gen. 6:8). That's it! That is God's only recorded motive. God saved Noah because He chose to save Noah.

God placed Noah and his family and all the animals safely in an ark and He shut them in (Gen. 7:16). God alone was the doorman! He saw to it that the door was closed securely and remained closed until all were safely deposited on the other side of the flood.

When the flood was over, Noah and his family and all the animals exited the ark safely on dry ground. Why? God guarded that door. Following the flood God promised never to destroy this world again—by water. He did not promise to never destroy this world again, however.

> Knowing this first: that scoffers will come in the last days, walking according to their own lusts, and saying, "Where is the promise of His coming? For since the fathers fell asleep, all things continue as they were from the beginning of creation." For this they willfully forget: that by the word of God the heavens were of old, and the earth standing out of water and in the water, by which the world that then existed perished, being flooded with water. (2 Pet. 3:3-5)

Scoffers are here today! They are asking, "Where is your God? What about His promise to once again engage this world with His judgment? Evil is rampant. Marriage between a man and woman is being threatened. Babies are being slaughtered by the millions. Drug cartels are flourishing. So where is your God?" they say.

Centuries have passed and still no Christ. Things continue to get worse. The scoffers are once again doing exactly what they did before Noah's flood.

God's judgment is coming once again. During Noah's time God quietly declared that it was going to rain. Surely not! It had never rained before. But it did (2 Pet. 3:5-6). As God predicted the flood in Noah's day, He has predicted that He is going to once again destroy this world. Not with water, but with fire.

> But the heavens and the earth which are now preserved by the same word are reserved for fire until the day of judgment and perdition of ungodly men. (2 Pet. 3:7)

Just as Noah and his family were spared from God's wrath by being positioned in the ark, those who will be spared from God's coming wrath must be positioned *in the body of Jesus Christ.* He is the ark for all Christians. Those who are "in Christ" will not perish. Once in Him, we can never get out of Him.

SEALED BY THE HOLY SPIRIT

Like God shut Noah and his family safely in the ark, He also shuts us safely *in Christ.* Let me explain!

There was no postal service in the ancient world. Important documents were sent by runners or men on horseback. Important letters had an official seal pressed upon the folds of the document. If the seal was broken for any reason before the letter was delivered, the carrier was arrested and punished, and the contents of the document rendered of no value. The seal could be broken only by the one to whom the letter was addressed.

In like manner, after believers are placed into Christ, God seals us in Him.

> In Him you also trusted, after you heard the word of truth, the gospel of your salvation; in whom also, having believed, you were sealed with the Holy Spirit of promise, who is the guarantee of our inheritance until the redemption of the purchased possession, to the praise of His glory. (Eph. 1:13-14)

The Christian's eternal salvation is guaranteed by this sealing ministry. Guarantee is the Greek word for "pledge," *arrobon.* It was often translated as "engagement ring." An engagement ring is a symbol that a promise will be kept.

God the Holy Spirit's seal becomes the *guarantee* that our position in Christ is forever secure.

> Now He who establishes us with you in Christ and anointed us is God, who also has sealed us and given

us the Spirit in our hearts as a guarantee. (2 Cor.
1:21-22)

By being "in Christ" we gain new life, His life (1 Jn. 5:11). We do
not receive probationary life or life until we sin again. A Christian
can never lose life that is eternal.

We do not keep ourselves saved by our weak human power; we
are kept by the power of God.

> Blessed be the God and Father of our Lord Jesus Christ,
> who according to His abundant mercy has begotten us
> again to a living hope through the resurrection of Jesus
> Christ from the dead, to an inheritance incorruptible and
> undefiled and that does not fade away, reserved in heaven
> for you, who are kept by the power of God through faith
> for salvation ready to be revealed in the last time. (1 Pet.
> 1:3-5)

It is God who holds on to us; we do not hold on to Him.

SEALED UNTIL

God guarded that door in the ark until all were safe on the other
side. We are sealed in Christ *until the redemption of the purchased
possession* (Eph. 1:14). *Redemption* means "to purchase from the
market by paying a price." We have been redeemed from the penalty
of sin because of our personal faith in Jesus Christ. We shall be
redeemed from the presence of sin when we receive our new bodies
by death or the rapture.

Until is a time word that signals the exact moment that God's
seal will be broken. This seal cannot be broken by anyone other
than the Lord Jesus Christ. He will not break it until the final
redemption of the body. He will not break it when we sin. He will
not break it when we fail to please Him and go our own way or run
contrary to His will.

We are not saved only until we sin again. We are not saved only until we fail to please God in some manner. We are saved until such time as we are redeemed from this fallen world by death or by the catching up of the church (1 Thess. 4:16-17). That is security that is eternal.

The Holy Spirit's seal is the guarantee that this future redemption of the body will take place.

> And not only this, but also we ourselves, having the first fruits of the Spirit, even we ourselves groan within ourselves, waiting eagerly for our adoption as sons, the redemption of our body. For in hope we have been saved, but hope that is seen is not hope; for who hopes for what he already sees? But if we hope for what we do not see, with perseverance we wait eagerly for it. (Rom. 8:23-25)

Jesus Christ left the planet with this promise ringing in the ears of His disciples:

> Let not your heart be troubled; you believe in God, believe also in Me. In My Father's house are many mansions; if it were not so, I would have told you. I go to prepare a place for you. And if I go and prepare a place for you, I will come again and receive you to Myself; that where I am, there you may be also. (Jn. 14:1-3)

Centuries have passed since He spoke these words. Has He forgotten His promise? No! Believers of every generation have looked for His coming. One day He will come and will take us home to be with Him.

A question arose among the believers in the church at Thessalonica because their loved ones had recently died. They began to ask whether or not they had missed the return of Christ and the catching up of the church. Paul answered their critical question this way:

> But I do not want you to be ignorant, brethren, concerning those who have fallen asleep lest you sorrow as others who

have no hope. For if we believe that Jesus died and rose again, even so God will bring with Him those who sleep in Jesus. (1 Thess. 4:13-14)

The word *hope,* when used in scripture, always points to the second coming of Jesus Christ. The *hope* of believers is the blessed assurance that Jesus Christ will come again. We do not hope that He will come back, but we hope that His coming will be soon.

When the believer dies, our human spirits (our souls) go to be with the Lord (2 Cor. 5:10). Our bodies go back to the earth from which they were made. When Jesus Christ returns, the human spirits of those who have died in Him will also return with Him. Only believers, those who sleep in Jesus, will be resurrected to be with Christ.

> For this we say to you by the word of the Lord, that we who are alive and remain until the coming of the Lord will by no means precede those who are asleep. For the Lord Himself will descend from heaven with a shout, with the voice of an archangel, and with the trumpet of God. And the dead in Christ will rise first. Then we who are alive and remain shall be caught up together with them in the clouds to meet the Lord in the air. And thus we shall always be with the Lord. Therefore comfort one another with these words. (1 Thess. 4:15-18)

Paul emphasized the importance of his teaching of the catching up of the church by saying that he spoke the words of the Lord. Believers who are living when Christ returns will not go up to meet Him before those who have died! Those who have gone through the valley of the shadow of death will be the first to meet the Lord. Then those who remain will be caught up to meet the resurrected saints and the Lord in the air.

The word *rapture* is not found in the Bible. We refer to the catching up of the saints as "the rapture" because "caught up together" in Latin is the word *raptura*. The glorified bodies of all believers who have died will be reunited with their living spirits.

The shout that will be heard that day may be a military command given by Michael, the commander of God's angelic army. From the rapture throughout eternity, all believers will forever be with the Lord.

We are made alive the moment we trust Jesus Christ as our Savior, but our bodies must also be transformed to conform to our new living spirits. Our fallen physical bodies are not designed for heaven. God must make that transformation also.

> Behold, I tell you a mystery: We shall not all sleep, but we shall all be changed—in a moment, in the twinkling of an eye, at the last trumpet. For the trumpet will sound, and the dead will be raised incorruptible, and we shall be changed. For this corruptible must put on incorruption, and this mortal must put on immortality. So when this corruptible has put on incorruption, and this mortal has put on immortality, then shall be brought to pass the saying that is written: "Death is swallowed up in victory." "O Death, where is your sting? O Hades, where is your victory?" The sting of death is sin, and the strength of sin is the law. But thanks be to God, who gives us the victory through our Lord Jesus Christ. Therefore, my beloved brethren, be steadfast, immovable, always abounding in the work of the Lord, knowing that your labor is not in vain in the Lord. (1 Cor. 15:51-58)

A *mystery,* in scripture, is a truth previously hidden in God that is now revealed. The mystery that is unveiled here is that not all believers will die physically. Some will be changed from their fallen physical bodies into their glorified bodies immediately. This transformation takes place in a moment at the twinkling of an eye. A *moment* is the smallest amount of divisible time. *The twinkling of an eye* is an idiom meaning "in the time it takes to recognize someone."

The trumpet is the same trumpet spoken of in 1 Thessalonians 4. Those who are resurrected from the dead will be changed, and those who are alive will be instantly transformed. Our human bodies will be changed that day into a body that is glorious (1 Cor. 15:35-45).

HELD TIGHT BY LOVE

Speaking of His sheep, Jesus said:

> My sheep hear My voice, and I know them, and they follow Me. And I give them eternal life, and they shall never perish; neither shall anyone snatch them out of My hand. My Father, who has given them to Me, is greater than all; and no one is able to snatch them out of My Father's hand. I and My Father are one. (Jn. 10:27-30)

Jesus Christ is holding all of His sheep in His hand, and no one is going to snatch them from Him. He holds on to us; we do not hold on to Him. He keeps us; we do not keep Him.

Our Lord went a step further. He said that His Father is the one who gave these sheep to the Christ, and His Father is the greatest of all. No one, repeat, no one is able to snatch the sheep out of His hand. That's security!

The book of Romans contains, arguably, the most important truth in the Bible concerning the personal salvation of the believer. Having finished the section explaining the grace of God that has been given to every Christian, Paul asked and answered seven questions that sum up the result to all that he had written from the book of Romans. He wrote, "What then shall we say to these things? If God is for us, who can be against us?" (Rom. 8:31).

Obviously, Satan and his demonic hosts from hell are against Christians, but they cannot ultimately triumph (Eph. 6:11-13; 1 Pet. 5:8). God is the sovereign creator, and Satan is but a creature. All creatures are under God's sovereign control. Since God is the one *for* us, no one in His created universe can oppose us successfully.

How do we know for sure that God is for us? Notice Paul's words, "He who did not spare His own Son, but delivered Him up for us all, how shall He not with Him also freely give us all things" (Rom. 8:32).

The word *spare* is the same word used in Genesis 22:12 when Abraham offered Isaac. God said to Abraham, "You have not withheld your son." Then God directed Abraham to spare Isaac and to offer a ram as a substitute (Gen. 22:2-14). God did not hold back His hand against His own Son, but He delivered Him up as a substitute for sin (Jn. 1:29). In view of this supreme act of God's grace, how will He not also with Him freely give us all things?

In offering His Son, He did the absolute most for us. Everything else falls under that. God can do no less for us now that we are in Christ.

Paul asked two more questions that involve God's justice when he wrote, "Who shall bring a charge against God's elect? It is God who justifies" (Rom. 8:33).

Charge is a legal word. Who has the power to press charges *against God's elect?* Satan is identified as "the accuser" of God's people (Job 1: 6-12). His accusations are valid, because they are based on the believer's sinfulness, but his accusations will be thrown out of court. Why? Because God is the one who justifies. God declares the elect in Christ Jesus justified because they are in His Son (Rom. 3:24; Phil. 3:9; 2 Cor. 5:21).

Paul continued, "Who is he who condemns? It is Christ who died, and furthermore is also risen, who is even at the right hand of God, who also makes intercession for us" (Rom. 8:35). This word *condemn* can have future sense: who will be able in the future to bring an accusation against the elect condemning any one of them?[7] No one!

Why is this true? Look at the presiding judge. Who is it? Why, the judge is the one who died for us and who was raised for our justification (Jn. 5:26-27). The judge is the Lord Jesus Christ. He is the one who is continuously interceding for us.

> Who shall separate us from the love of Christ? Shall tribulation, or distress, or persecution, or famine, or nakedness, or peril, or sword? As it is written: "For Your sake we are killed all day long; we are accounted as sheep for the slaughter." Yet in all these things we are more than conquerors through Him who loved us. (Rom. 8:35-37)

The *love of Christ* is His love for believers not their love for Him. Paul suggested seven possibilities that could give the believer the impression that Christ really does not love us and has abandoned us.

- Tribulation (trouble; pressure)
- Distress (being hemmed in on every side; being pressed into a corner)
- Persecution (being persecuted for our faith)
- Famine (starvation)
- Nakedness (having no clothes)
- Peril (facing danger)
- Sword (facing death)

Each of these possibilities increases in intensity. The list starts with something fairly light and ends by facing the king of terror–death! These are things that many believers in the first three centuries of Christianity faced with regularity.

Rather than being separated from Christ's love, we overwhelmingly conquer. This is the ultimate goal of the believer's sanctification.

> But thanks be to God, who always leads us in triumph in Christ, and manifests through us the sweet aroma of the knowledge of Him in every place. (2 Cor. 2:14, NASB)

Paul's next list begins where the previous list ended. This list begins with death and covers every possible sphere of existence and vast extremes in every dominion. He concluded:

> For I am persuaded that neither death nor life, nor angels
> nor principalities nor powers, nor things present nor things
> to come, nor height nor depth, nor any other created thing,
> shall be able to separate us from the love of God which is
> in Christ Jesus our Lord. (Rom. 8:38-39)

- Neither death nor life: two extremes that face us. Death will not separate us; life will not disconnect us.
- Nor angels nor principalities: two extremes in the angelic realm. Angels, good or bad, cannot separate us.
- Nor things present nor things to come: extremes in anything that is known now or extremes in that which may be anticipated in the future.
- Nor powers: satanic power and demons, human governments, some power in space that we do not know about.
- Nor height nor depth: nothing from up above as far as one could go and nothing underneath, or down below.
- Nor any other created thing: nothing in the entire created realm.
- Will be able to separate us from the love of God, which is in Christ Jesus our Lord: absolutely nothing in His creation can thwart God's purpose for believers in Christ.

What a climactic way to end the certainty of believers' justification and sanctification.

As Noah and family were safe in that ark, all who have trusted Jesus Christ as Savior are forever safe in Him. Eternal life is available to those who trust the Lord Jesus Christ as Savior. The life that is provided to the believer at the moment of faith is forever life. Eternal life is just that, life that will never end. Those who have truly believed in Christ can never be lost.

CHAPTER 7

A GLIMPSE OF THE CHRISTIAN'S WALK

Christians are by their very nature people of faith. We are given life from God by faith, and we are to live our entire lives on earth by faith. Paul said it like this: "For we walk by faith, not by sight" (2 Cor. 5:7).

What did Paul mean by walking by faith and not sight? Catch this glimpse! Walking is an interesting physical movement. We move forward into the walking motion by pushing off on one leg and then shifting our weight to the other. Our weight is transferred from one leg to another as we move along. By faith, with every step we take, we release our weight, first on one leg and then the other. There is a brief moment when we must trust that the coming leg will hold us up. When we are small, we take short, unsteady steps, but as we grow older we take longer and surer steps. This is the ideal illustration of living by faith.

Walking by faith is placing our spiritual weight upon the word of God, moment by moment, throughout our lives. At first we take small steps of faith, trusting God for small things. But as we mature in Christ, we take larger steps of faith, trusting God for more important things. God teaches us to do this.

Moses told the Jews that God had humbled them, allowing them to go hungry in the wilderness so that He could supply their need. He fed them with manna in order to show them that man shall not live by bread alone but that man lives by every word that comes from the mouth of God. When God gave them this supernatural food, He specifically instructed them to take only what they needed for that day, no more. God was teaching them to trust Him for their daily food. They were to learn to take God at His word. God will be faithful! They were to learn to walk by faith.

Jesus appealed to this truth in His response to Satan's temptation when He said, "It is written, 'Man shall not live by bread alone, but by every word that proceeds from the mouth of God'" (Matt. 4:4). Walking by faith is learning to live our lives here on this earth, not by sight, but by knowing and obeying God's Word.

Paul was growing old. His body was wearing out, but that which was going on inside him–in his spirit–grew stronger with each passing day.

> Therefore we do not lose heart. Even though our outward man is perishing, yet the inward man is being renewed day by day. For our light affliction, which is but for a moment, is working for us a far more exceeding and eternal weight of glory. (2 Cor. 4:16-17)

What was this momentary light affliction? Paul mentioned a part of this affliction later in this very book.

> In labors more abundant, in stripes above measure, in prisons more frequently, in deaths often. From the Jews five times I received forty stripes minus one. Three times I was beaten with rods; once I was stoned; three times I was shipwrecked; a night and a day I have been in the deep; in journeys often, in perils of waters, in perils of robbers, in perils of my own countrymen, in perils of the Gentiles, in perils in the city, in perils in the wilderness, in perils in

the sea, in perils among false brethren; in weariness and toil, in sleeplessness often, in hunger and thirst, in fastings often, in cold and nakedness–besides the other things, what comes upon me daily: my deep concern for all the churches. (2 Cor. 11:23-28)

This is momentary light affliction? Compared to the exceeding and eternal weight of glory awaiting Paul beyond this world, it was. Paul wrote that the fleeting trials that we face here are crushed by the weight of the glory that awaits us! He then told us how to strengthen our faith in the things to come.

While we do not look at the things which are seen, but at the things which are not seen. For the things which are seen are temporary, but the things which are not seen are eternal. (2 Cor. 4:18)

We are not to look on the things that are seen. What does this mean? We do not put our confidence in the visible things that are locked in time and space in this physical world. We are not to build our lives by becoming attached to the stuff in this life. Why? Because all that is seen with the eyes is said to be temporary and destined to perish.

In contrast, we are to look at things that are not seen. The things that are not seen are eternal things existing in God's spiritual world. They are heavenly things such as a living Savior, a heavenly home, and the existence of a heavenly body that awaits us. In contrast to the passing physical things of this life, these are eternal things. These are things that we believe by faith.

Paul spent his entire life being taught by God! His view of heavenly things became so real to him that it became his motivation for living. He clarified one of these spiritual truths for us when he said, "For we know that if our earthly house, this tent, is destroyed, we have a building from God, a house not made with hands, eternal in the heavens" (2 Cor. 5:1).

The earthly tent of which Paul spoke is our physical body. If our body goes back to the dust from which it was made, God will give us a new body. This must be believed by faith.

Paul continued to explain that "we groan in this earthly body, desiring to be clothed with our body that is from heaven." We crave this new body. He summed it all up with these words: "For we walk by faith, not by sight…" (2 Cor. 5:8).

Walking by faith does not mean making life's decisions by the whims of our human inclinations or our human emotions. It is not charting the course of our lives by listening to and heeding strange voices or responding to clairvoyant visions. It is not reading into the Bible our thoughts or interpretations. Walking by faith does not mean wandering around through life, taking unknown leaps into the dark.

Walking by faith is working hard to understand the clear teaching of God's word and allowing the Spirit to unravel for us the divine wisdom found there. We then submit our human wills to what is written. The Bible is the absolute source of our faith. Paul's words come to mind again.

> Faith comes by hearing and hearing by the word of God.
> (Rom. 10:17)

There is no substitute for studying, living, and teaching the Bible. The more time we spend in the Bible, the more we begin to trust God's word for guidance, and the stronger our faith becomes.

A friend once shared with me that the most terrifying thing he had ever done was fly an airplane by instruments. He spent months learning how to use them. He worked hard imagining what it would be like to depend solely on the many gauges and dials in front of him. He said the first time he actually put in action what he had learned was a heart-wrenching moment. He took off from the airport, and for the first time had to fly into the clouds at over 300 miles per hour. He could see nothing through the windshield of the aircraft.

At first he felt the overwhelming tendency to panic and revert back to flying the airplane by sight. He steadied himself and focused in on the instrument panel in front of him. The instruments were all he had to tell him how fast he was flying, how high he was flying, whether he was right side up or upside down, or in what direction he was going. It was exciting as well as extremely scary!

Operating by the instruments alone, he came out of the clouds, hoping that the airport was where the instruments said it was supposed to be. And there it was! What a deep feeling of relief. Success after success taught him that he could rely on the airplane's capability. The airport was always there.

That accurately describes how Christians learn to live by faith. By taking small steps of faith, we learn to rely upon the sound teaching of God's Word, not our own human wishes. God's word often goes contrary to our human desires and tendencies. It tells us to serve those that we wish to lead. Our success is found not through self-promoting pride and arrogance but through submission and humility.

My pilot friend said that when flying by instruments he could not allow himself to revert back to what his human inclinations were telling him for even a moment. He had to train himself to depend solely on the instruments. The same is true when living by God's Word. As we learn to walk by faith, we discover that God's airport is always where it is supposed to be. God is always faithful to do what He said He would do. We can trust Him with our very lives.

As the disciples spent personal time with Jesus Christ every day, their faith grew. They walked with Him and talked with Him and learned to put their confidence in Him. They grew to love Him. We can do the same thing today–by faith.

- By faith we can attend the wedding at Cana in Galilee where the Christ turned the water into wine.

- By faith we can sit beside Him in the boat on the Sea of Galilee when He stilled the storm with the words, "Peace, be still."
- By faith we can observe the faces of the blind man that the Christ caused to see, the leper that He cleansed, and we can rejoice with the crippled man as he walked for the first time in his life.
- By faith we can stand with Him, under the sycamore tree when Jesus called old Zacchaeus to himself.
- By faith we can be there as He cursed the fig tree and as He talked with the woman of Samaria.
- By faith we can stand with Him and sense His grief as He wept at the death of His friend, but then we can stand amazed when He called Lazarus to life.
- By faith we can observe Him on the cross as He cried out, "My God, My God why have your forsaken me?"
- By faith we can hear Him say, "Father, forgive them for they know not what they are doing."
- By faith we can stand by the two Marys at the mouth of His empty tomb and hear the angels say, "He is not here, for He has risen as He said He would."
- By faith we can walk with Him along the road to Emmaus following His resurrection.
- By faith we can touch His resurrected body as Thomas did.

WALK WORTHY OF THE LORD

> For this reason we also, since the day we heard it, do not cease to pray for you, and to ask that you may be filled with the knowledge of His will in all wisdom and spiritual understanding; that you may walk worthy of the Lord, fully pleasing Him. (Col. 1:9-10)

What does Paul mean by walking "worthy of the Lord, fully pleasing Him"? An illustration is the best answer. In Matthew

14:24-33, we see that Jesus Christ took a walk out on the waters of the Sea of Galilee. He could do this because He created that sea. He walked up close to the disciples' boat and spoke to them, "Be of good cheer! It is I; do not be afraid."

Peter decided to join Christ on the water. He said, "Lord, if it is You, command me to come to You on the water."

Jesus extended a single word invitation: "Come!" Peter bailed out of the boat and onto the water. At first he enjoyed his walk with the Savior. He had his eyes fixed on Jesus Christ and therefore he walked on the water.

Suddenly Peter became aware of what was going on around him. He felt the wind and saw the waves. Immediately he began to sink and cried out, "Lord, save me!"

Jesus reached out His hand and caught Him saying, "O you of little faith, why did you doubt?" When they got into the boat, the wind ceased (Matt. 14:31).

Peter had the amazing power to walk on the water as long as he kept his eyes fixed on Jesus Christ. This is the very basis for living the Christian life. Walking worthy of the Lord is cultivating a close, personal, private, intimate relationship with the Lord Jesus Christ.

The Lord Jesus is at this moment in heaven seated at the Father's right hand. It is from that vantage point that He fulfills His ministry as our eternal High Priest.

> Now this is the main point of the things we are saying: We have such a High Priest, who is seated at the right hand of the throne of the Majesty in the heavens, a Minister of the sanctuary and of the true tabernacle which the Lord erected, and not man. (Heb. 8:1-2)

> Seeing then that we have a great High Priest who has passed through the heavens, Jesus the Son of God, let us hold fast our confession. For we do not have a High Priest who cannot sympathize with our weaknesses, but was in all points tempted as we are, yet without sin. Let

us therefore come boldly to the throne of grace that we
may obtain mercy and find grace to help in time of need.
(Heb. 4:14-16)

Christians on the earth are a group of believer priests cultivating
a spiritual relationship with our High Priest in heaven (1 Pet. 2:5).
Living the Christian life means spending quality time with Him, thus
growing to understand His will for us. It means allowing Him to talk
to us through His word and talking with Him in prayer.

Also there were many priests, because they were prevented
by death from continuing. But He, because He continues
forever, has an unchangeable priesthood. Therefore He is
also able to save to the uttermost those who come to God
through Him, since He always lives to make intercession
for them. (Heb. 7:23-25)

This is the life of faith! This was Paul's prayer for the believers
at Ephesus:

So that Christ may dwell in your hearts through faith;
and that you, being rooted and grounded in love, may be
able to comprehend with all the saints what is the breadth
and length and height and depth, and to know the love of
Christ which surpasses knowledge, that you may be filled
up to all the fullness of God. (Eph. 3:17-19)

NOT RULES BUT RELATIONSHIP

Public enemy number one to the Christian's walk with Christ
in Paul's mind was not drugs or alcohol, as devastating as they can
be. Nor was his enemy abortion, euthanasia, pornography, divorce,
sexual immorality, or a corrupt government. Paul feared legalism
above all else.

Most of the people coming to faith in Christ in the early years of
Christianity were Jews. They were saved out of a spiritually bankrupt

system called Judaism. They had grown up in that system and it had a tremendous fleshly appeal to them.

Judaism consisted of meetings in elaborate buildings draped in beautiful cloth with furniture trimmed in gold. It also involved religious ceremonies with ornate costumes, attending the temple three times a day, public reading of the law, singing, impressive public prayers, breathtaking sacrificial ceremonies with the smell of the burning altar, and religious festivals.

Days were filled with good times with family and friends. Deep under the outward ceremony, however, were the cold realities of law. Paul had been raised in Judaism. He knew that all the so-called "service of God" rituals were strictly that–rituals. They had no real spiritual impact on anyone. People went through the motions with no spiritual meaning at all.

This system of religion contained far more bondage than the tar pits of Egypt. Jesus said this of the religious legalists of His day:

> Woe to you, scribes and Pharisees, hypocrites! For you are like whitewashed tombs which indeed appear beautiful outwardly, but inside are full of dead men's bones and all uncleanness. Even so you also outwardly appear righteous to men, but inside you are full of hypocrisy and lawlessness. (Matt. 23:27-28)

Some trusted Jesus Christ and were born of God. They experienced absolute freedom from the guilt and penalty of their sin (Rom. 3:24). They were connected to Jesus Christ by a new birth, by position, and by possession. They had been transformed!

Many of these new Christians failed to grow in their relationships with Christ. There was a strong tendency to go back to the rituals and the beautiful ceremonies to which they had become accustomed. Paul realized that this was Satan's trap. It is a quicksand from which few escaped. Paul taught them to not go back to the old law system but to go on with Christ.

> Or do you not know, brethren (for I speak to those who know the law), that the law has dominion over a man as long as he lives? (Rom. 7:1)

The law's spiritual dominance is only for those who are alive. What strange words! But they are true. The spiritual cursing power of God's law has never been abolished. The Holy Spirit uses this power to convict of sin and draw unbelievers to faith in Christ. We realize that we have sinned and come short of the glory of God because the Holy Spirit convinces us that we have not kept God's commandments. Once convicting us of our sin, the law then points us to Christ where there is cleansing and life (Gal. 3:13).

Paul said that the law was "our tutor to bring us to Christ, that we might be justified by faith" (Gal. 3:24). The word *tutor* means "schoolmaster." A schoolmaster in the ancient world took the children to school, looked after them, and then brought them home again. The law is God's schoolmaster to bring us to Christ.

Paul continued, "But after faith has come, we are no longer under a tutor" (Gal. 3:25). Once we have been brought to Christ, we are never to go back to living the Christian life by means of the Mosaic Law. In fact, we are not to live the Christian life by any set of religious rules or regulations. This is legalism! Legalism is the attempt to live the Christian life based on a self-imposed system of "do this and don't do that." The motivation for keeping these rules becomes self-righteousness, or glorifying self through religious ritualism.

A person who is living in legalism has conformed to a set of personal traditions and may think he or she is pleasing God. The feeling is, "If I go to church regularly, sing in the choir, give my money, and don't drink, smoke, chew, or dance, then I'm okay." The Bible tells us that there is an *appearance of wisdom* in feeling this way.

> Therefore, if you died with Christ to the basic principles of the world, why, as though you were living in the world, do you subject yourselves to regulations–"Do not touch, do not taste, do not handle," which all concern things which perish with the using–according to the commandments and doctrines of men? These things indeed have an appearance of wisdom in self-imposed religion, false humility, and neglect of the body, but are of no value against the indulgence of the flesh. (Col. 2:20-23)

These "doctrines of men" may make us feel good about ourselves spiritually. Paul warned, "For we dare not class ourselves or compare ourselves with those who commend themselves. But they, measuring themselves by themselves, and comparing themselves among themselves, are not wise" (2 Cor. 10:12).

Living a legalistic lifestyle produces pride and the lust for the praise of others. Works performed or temptations denied can be a product of self-reformation. A person whose life is built on a faulty foundation of human traditionalism and personal convictions and not upon the word of God will seldom come to understand what it means to walk by faith and not by sight.

This lifestyle becomes so ingrained, so much a part of life that we become blind to our personal walk with Jesus Christ. Legalism becomes a subtle substitute for a pure, simple relationship with the all-knowing, all-powerful, unchangeable living God. This, my friend, is why Paul feared legalism so.

Morality is not always to be equated with Christianity. Many religious people throughout the world are very moral people. They do myriads of good things for others. In fact, many atheists and agnostics, who are disciplined and governed by various personal codes of ethics, demonstrate morality without ever being religious at all.

In many communities throughout the world, the most moral people on the block are not Christians. Don't misunderstand! Christians should be the very best people on the planet, but being a good person and doing religious things does not make anyone a Christian.

The death, burial, and resurrection of Jesus Christ marked an end to all the rituals of the law. Many Jewish believers, however, had the tendency to gravitate back into this religious climate, but Paul taught them to *go on with Christ.*

DEAD TO LAW

Paul gave a simple but understandable illustration of the law's spiritual power.

> For the woman who has a husband is bound by the law to her husband as long as he lives. But if the husband dies, she is released from the law of her husband. So then if, while her husband lives, she marries another man, she will be called an adulteress; but if her husband dies, she is free from that law, so that she is no adulteress, though she has married another man. (Rom. 7:2-3)

The law binds a woman to her husband as long as he is alive, but if he dies the woman is free to remarry. We have no trouble understanding this principle. Paul then applied this very truth to our relationship with Christ. He continued, "Therefore, my brethren, you also have become dead to the law through the body of Christ" (Rom. 7:4). Paul's application is crystal clear. Since we died in Christ, the spirit of the law has no jurisdiction over us.

Before Christ, the law exercised its spiritual power, reminding us that we are sinners. But once we believe and are identified with Christ, the law's condemning power is forever broken.

Suppose a man has committed a murder resulting in the death penalty. He is arrested and brought into the court before the judge and indicted. The witnesses are called and, one by one, they testify against him. There seems to be no defense at all. He is guilty as charged and sentenced to death. But before the sentence can be carried out, he suddenly grasps his throat, stiffens, and dies. The coroner is called, and he pronounces that the criminal is officially, legally dead.

Now what does the judge do? Does he continue with the trial? Of course not! The law cannot try a dead man. The man is beyond the reach of the law. The judge raps his gavel on his desk and pronounces, "Case closed!"[8]

Amazingly the man is resurrected. He is seen very much alive. Someone shouts, "Quick, go get the sheriff!" The man is hauled in before the judge. The judge checks the books, and the books say that he is dead. Since he is legally dead, the law has no jurisdiction over him.[9]

Likewise, all believers have died to the spiritual effect of the law. Where did we die? We died in Christ.

> Do you not know that as many of us as were baptized into Christ Jesus were baptized into His death? (Rom. 6:3).

In fact, we have also been raised in Christ.

> But God, who is rich in mercy, because of His great love with which He loved us, even when we were dead in trespasses, made us alive together with Christ (by grace you have been saved), and raised us up together, and made us sit together in the heavenly places in Christ Jesus. (Eph. 2:4-6)

What a glimpse of God's grace! This is truth that must be taken by faith but real truth nonetheless. God designed the law for a particular purpose, but that purpose does not apply to a resurrected person. We are free from the law.

ALIVE TO CHRIST

One can almost hear the shouts now! "No law? How is it possible to live the Christian life without law? What would prevent us from freefalling into sin and living vile sinful lives?"

Remember that grace teaches us to live soberly, righteously, and godly in this present age (Titus 2:11-12). How is it possible for believers to live a right lifestyle?

> That you may be married to another–to Him who was raised from the dead. (Rom. 7:4b)

Christians are married to Jesus Christ! Paul said, "For I am jealous for you with a godly jealousy, for I betrothed you to one husband, that to Christ I might present you as a pure virgin" (2 Cor. 11:2).

A good illustration of our relationship to Jesus Christ is the marriage of a Christian husband and wife.

> But as the church is subject to Christ, so also the wives ought to be to their husbands in everything. Husbands, love your wives, just as Christ also loved the church and gave Himself up for her; that He might sanctify her, having cleansed her by the washing of water with the word, that He might present to Himself the church in all her glory, having no spot or wrinkle or any such thing; but that she should be holy and blameless. (Eph. 5:24-27)

When my wife and I married, we became one flesh. This truth is so important that God repeats it over and over in His word (Gen. 2:24; Matt. 19:5-6; 1 Cor. 6:16; Eph. 5:31). How do I want my own flesh treated? Very well, thank you! I do not please my wife out of obligation. I want to please her because she is a part of me.

Likewise, I am one with Jesus Christ. I am a part of His body. For that reason, I want to please Him. Our relationship with Christ places us on a higher plane than any law ever could. I have no desire to do things that would displease Christ, and I want to do things that will please Him.

Christians serve Christ not through keeping rules but through a personal relationship. This relationship involves obedience to Him. He tells us to keep His commandment of loving one another and to abide in His word (Jn. 13:34). The motivation to do this is not the coldness of the law but the warmth and tenderness of love.

When we trust Jesus Christ as Savior, we belong to Him. As we begin to grow in this relationship, stimulated by a study of His Word, our love for the Lord Jesus Christ grows. As our love for Him increases, so should our desire to please Him in our thoughts, our words, and our ways. We should have no problem making decisions about what we are to watch or what words we are to listen to or what we put into our bodies. We should be motivated to please the one who bought us with His precious blood (Lk. 6:46).

> If anyone loves Me, he will keep My word; and My Father will love him, and We will come to him and make our home with him. He who does not love Me does not keep My words; and the word which you hear is not Mine but the Father's who sent Me. (Jn. 14:23-24)

WALK IN THE SPIRIT

> I say then: Walk in the Spirit, and you shall not fulfill the lust of the flesh. (Gal. 5:16)

Nothing that comes from the flesh of man has ever pleased God. God will not bless self-righteous efforts in the slightest way. He will bless only what He does through us. Christians are to serve God, energized by the Holy Spirit. Paul said that we have been "delivered from the law, having died to what we were held by, so that we should serve in the newness of the Spirit and not in the oldness of the letter" (Rom. 7:6).

The Holy Spirit alone gives us the necessary power to live a life pleasing to God. In fact, Paul said that we are to be filled with the Spirit.

> And do not get drunk with wine, for that is dissipation, but be filled with the Spirit. (Eph. 5:18)

The Spirit's filling ministry is severely misunderstood. Some misguided people teach that His filling is a second work of His grace whereby God anoints Christians, in some way empowering them to serve Him.

What exactly is the filling of the Holy Spirit? In order to understand this filling ministry, we need to compare Ephesians 5 with Colossians 3, which are parallel passages from the pen of Paul. Notice first in Ephesians 5 the result of the Spirit's filling.

> Speaking to one another in psalms and hymns and spiritual songs, singing and making melody in your heart to the Lord, giving thanks always for all things to God the Father in the name of our Lord Jesus Christ, submitting to one another in the fear of God. Wives, submit to your own husbands, as to the Lord. For the husband is head of the wife, as also Christ is head of the church; and He is the Savior of the body. Therefore, just as the church is subject to Christ, so let the wives be to their own husbands in everything. (Eph. 5:19-24)

Look closely at the parallel text in Colossians 3.

> Let the word of Christ dwell in you richly in all wisdom, teaching and admonishing one another in psalms and hymns and spiritual songs, singing with grace in your hearts to the Lord. And whatever you do in word or deed, do all in the name of the Lord Jesus, giving thanks to God the Father through Him. Wives, submit to your own husbands, as is fitting in the Lord. Husbands, love

your wives and do not be bitter toward them. Children, obey your parents in all things, for this is well pleasing to the Lord. Fathers, do not provoke your children, lest they become discouraged. (Col. 3:16-21)

In Ephesians Paul said, "Be filled with the Spirit," and in Colossians, "Let the word of Christ dwell in you richly." The results, however, are exactly the same in both cases: singing songs and hymns, submission and a thankful heart. Therefore, we can conclude that letting the word of Christ dwell in you richly is the very same act as being filled with the Spirit.

"Be filled with the Spirit" in Ephesians literally means, "Be being filled with the Spirit." It means that we are to put ourselves in the position to be utilized by the Holy Spirit of God. We are to maintain a personal walk with Jesus Christ. As we continue to do this, we place ourselves at the discretion of the Holy Spirit to use us as He pleases.

When God chooses to magnify Christ through us, He will do so. At that moment the Spirit of God will control us. It may be to share the gospel with someone, or communicate a truth from His word or answer a question, sing a song–whatever. We can never demand to be controlled by God's Spirit. He controls us. We do not choose the times or the places; God does. Our part is to be a usable vessel.

CHAPTER 8

A GLIMPSE OF THE CHRISTIAN'S WORKS

Christians are saved by grace alone, through faith alone, in Jesus Christ alone.

> For by grace you have been saved through faith and that not of yourselves. It is the gift of God not of works lest any man should boast. (Eph. 2:8-9)

Human works have no part in our salvation. If a single work is added to the work of Christ for salvation, grace is nullified and life will not come (Rom. 4:4-5).

However, we are saved by faith in order to work for the God that saved us. Works do not save, but we are saved to work. Christians are not given God's life to simply sit in a pew and listen to a sermon.

Someone has accurately said, "Christianity is not a spectator sport." Christians are saved to glorify God within the generation in which they live. To glorify is to "shed light upon." Said simply, Christians are saved to serve. Every Christian has a divine destiny to fulfill.

Though we cannot work *for* our salvation, the faith that saves us will be productive. The very next words after Paul's declaration that we are saved by grace through faith attest to that fact.

> For we are His workmanship, created in Christ Jesus for good works, which God prepared beforehand, that we should walk in them. (Eph. 2:10, NASB)

We were created in Christ for the purpose of walking in good works. Notice that God even prepares the works that we will do. He works in us, executing that which pleases Him (Phil. 2:12-13).

James said that "as the body without the spirit is dead, so faith without works is dead also" (Jas. 2:26). Was James contradicting Paul's teaching that we are saved by grace alone? No!

Follow the context of what James was teaching. Just prior to writing this section, he had taken believers to task for treating the wealthy differently than they treated the poor. They ushered the rich people down front in their meetings, giving them the best seats, but the poor had to take what was left. James appealed to the believers to reach out to the poor among them (Jas. 2:1-5). In fact, he insinuated that how they treated the poor revealed the kind of faith they had. Dead faith is faith that does not produce.

> What use is it, my brethren, if someone says he has faith but he has no works? Can that faith save him? (Jas. 2:14)

James used an illustration pointing directly to the unbelieving, arrogant Jews who said they had faith in God yet made no attempt to meet the physical needs of poor Christians. This religious crowd, when approached by believers in desperate need of clothes or food, responded with words like, "We'll pray for you, brother." They made no attempt to help. They were good with their words, but they were always careful to separate themselves from the Christians in need. This self-righteous crowd said that they believed in "one God," indicating that they felt the Christians wrongly believed that Jesus

Christ is God. Yet their works spoke so loudly that it was obvious that they had not exercised saving faith. James emphasized that faith that does not produce works is not saving faith.

James reminded these religious hypocrites that the demons also believed in God–and trembled (Jas. 2:19). The demons obviously are not saved. To profess belief in one God is good theology, but it is not saving faith. Saving faith must be placed in the right object, the Lord Jesus Christ.

He went on to illustrate his point by saying that the way believers show their living faith is by treating the poor fairly.

> If a brother or sister is naked and destitute of daily food, and one of you says to them, "Depart in peace, be warmed and filled," but you do not give them the things which are needed for the body, what *does it* profit? Thus also faith by itself, if it does not have works, is dead. But someone will say, "You have faith, and I have works." Show me your faith without your works, and I will show you my faith by my works. You believe that there is one God. You do well. Even the demons believe—and tremble! But do you want to know, O foolish man, that faith without works is dead? (Jas. 2:15-20)

James was not teaching that we are given life from God by faith plus works. God will produce works in the lives of those who possess the right kind of faith. A living faith in Jesus Christ will be a productive faith.

That is exactly what Paul said in Eph. 2:10. Believers were created in Christ for the purpose of producing good works. The germinated seed of the gospel will produce God's life in the believer, and this life will produce fruit. This is at the heart of what James taught.

ABRAHAM'S FAITH WORK

James immediately gave two clear illustrations that saving faith will be productive.

> Was not Abraham justified by works when he offered Isaac
> his son on the altar? (Jas. 2:21)

Remember, Abraham received a right standing before God by faith and faith alone (Gen. 15:6). We discovered in *A Glimpse of the Christ* that the object of Abraham's faith was the Lord Jesus Christ. He believed in Jehovah. Jehovah of the Old Testament is Jesus Christ of the New Testament. Abraham's faith righteousness becomes the pattern for all of us (Gal. 3:5-13; Rom. 4:1-5; Jas. 2:23). Human works did not justify Abraham before God; his justification *came only by faith.* But what about Abraham's faith work?

God had promised Abraham and Sarah a son. Abraham grew old and Sarah was barren. After trying to help God help them, they finally had to rest all their hope on God. He responded by miraculously giving Sarah a son. A few years later, God put Abraham through one of the most severe tests that any human could endure. He asked Abraham to make an offering, not of an animal but of his most cherished possession, his son. This seemed completely irrational from man's perspective; but Abraham's obedience proved that he had placed his faith in the living God.

Abraham rose up early in the morning, took Isaac, and departed to do what God had instructed him to do. Evidently there was no reluctance and no second thoughts. Just before Abraham was to take his son's life, God miraculously stepped into the picture and spared Isaac (Heb. 11:17). But in Abraham's mind, he had actually taken the boy's life.

Abraham's offering of Isaac was the work of his faith. It was the work that God had planned for him to perform millions of years before Abraham was born (Eph. 2:10). That work confirmed that his faith was genuine (Jas. 2:14). The act of offering Isaac did not justify Abraham before God, but offering Isaac was clear evidence that Abraham had truly exercised saving faith (Jas. 2:22).

RAHAB'S FAITH WORK

James continued with another illustration.

> Likewise, was not Rahab the harlot also justified by works when she received the messengers and sent them out another way? (Jas. 2:25)

Rahab also illustrated that saving faith is productive faith. The Jews had left Egypt, winding their way to Canaan. They came to a small bump in the road called Kadesh Barnea. There they had a committee meeting. They decided to send twelve spies into Canaan to see what they were up against. In the city of Jericho some of the spies were discovered and the authorities attempted to capture them. A harlot named Rahab hid the spies, sparing them from certain death. God amazingly used this woman–a harlot of all people–to preserve the entire Jewish nation. This was her work of faith (Heb. 11:31).

There is no written record that Rahab had ever believed in the Lord as Abraham had, but she obviously did. Why? Her faith work proved it. She hid the spies *because* she had believed in the Lord. Her work revealed that her faith was a living faith in the living God. The seed of the word of God in her had produced fruit after its kind.

Both James and Paul were right! Personal faith in Jesus Christ is the root of our salvation. After we believe, God leaves us in this world to produce fruit for His glory. Good works become proof that the seed of the gospel has been germinated in us. God has foreordained it to be so.

Our works may not be giving to the poor as they were in James' day. In fact, attempting to recognize the work of faith in our lives and in the lives of others is futile. We are never given the responsibility to inspect the fruit in the lives of others. God alone knows when, where, and how our faith will become productive. We see this divine formula being played out through the list of faithful believers found in Hebrews 11.

THE EVIDENCE OF FAITH

> Now faith is the substance of things hoped for, the evidence
> of things not seen. (Heb. 11:1)

The writer of Hebrews said that faith is the substance of things hoped for. John MacArthur said that faith is living in a hope that is so real that it gives us great confidence for the future.[10] This hope becomes the evidence of things not seen. Abraham's entire life was lived by faith.

> By faith Abraham obeyed when he was called to go out to
> the place which he would receive as an inheritance. And
> he went out, not knowing where he was going. By faith
> he dwelt in the land of promise as in a foreign country,
> dwelling in tents with Isaac and Jacob, the heirs with
> him of the same promise; for he waited for the city which
> has foundations, whose builder and maker is God. (Heb.
> 11:8-10)

Abraham left his home in Chaldea to follow the living God by faith. He received his inheritance in Canaan by faith. He lived in a tent his entire life, but he looked for a city whose builder and maker is God. He trusted in the word of God and not what he could see.

Noah also trusted in the unseen when he heard God's word and believed Him. How do we know that he believed God? By faith he built an ark. He believed that it was going to rain, and his faith motivated him to work. Board by board, for 120 years he proclaimed the truth of the unseen living God to everyone around by performing his work of faith.

God says that the only way to please Him is by faith.

> But without faith it is impossible to please Him, for he
> who comes to God must believe that He is, and that He is
> a rewarder of those who diligently seek Him. (Heb. 11:6)

You might be thinking, *If God would only give me some visible proof, then I would believe and follow Christ,* but faith does not need visible proof. Faith does not need sight or touch. God has given us His Word. By faith we are to seek to understand what He has said to us and by faith we are to do what God tells us to do.

The writer of Hebrews 11 highlighted several Old Testament saints, giving testimony to their living faith. Each one, like Abraham, was given few details, but they put their trust and hope in the teaching that God gave them. That defines the substance of faith. Though many lived and died without seeing the reality behind their faith, they put their confidence in God's word nonetheless.

Note the work of faith of these Old Testament saints:

- By faith Abel offered a better sacrifice than Cain.
- By faith Enoch was taken away.
- By faith Noah prepared an ark.
- By faith Abraham obeyed and went out.
- By faith Sarah received strength to conceive seed.
- By faith Abraham offered up Isaac.
- By faith Isaac blessed Jacob and Esau.
- By faith Jacob blessed Joseph's sons and worshipped.
- By faith Joseph gave instructions concerning his bones.
- By faith Moses refused to be called the son of Pharaoh's daughter but esteemed the reproaches of Christ greater than the riches of Egypt.
- By faith the walls of Jericho fell down.
- By faith the harlot Rahab did not perish with those who did not believe.

The writer continues:

> And what more shall I say? For the time would fail me to tell of Gideon and Barak and Samson and Jephthah, also of David and Samuel and the prophets: who through

faith subdued kingdoms, worked righteousness, obtained promises, stopped the mouths of lions, quenched the violence of fire, escaped the edge of the sword, out of weakness were made strong, became valiant in battle, turned to flight the armies of the aliens. Women received their dead raised to life again. Others were tortured, not accepting deliverance, that they might obtain a better resurrection. Still others had trial of mockings and scourgings, yes, and of chains and imprisonment. They were stoned, they were sawn in two, were tempted, were slain with the sword. They wandered about in sheepskins and goatskins, being destitute, afflicted, tormented–of whom the world was not worthy. They wandered in deserts and mountains, in dens and caves of the earth. (Heb. 11:32-38)

The scripture never gives any details concerning the saving faith of most of these people, but we know that the root of faith was there because we read of the fruit that their faith produced. All of the faith testimonies had one common link.

Catch this glimpse! Their faith's work all blended together to achieve one goal. The target was to get Jesus Christ to Calvary and to the empty tomb. Abel pictured Him. Enoch pictured Him. Noah and the ark pictured Him. Abraham's offering of Isaac pictured Him. Jacob's ladder pictured Him. Joseph pictured Him. In a remarkable sense, they all–like Abraham–had Jesus Christ as an object of their faith.

This is why Moses, long before Christ came, considered the reproach of Christ greater than the riches of Egypt (Heb. 11:26). His Messiah was not to come for 1400 more years. Now that's faith! God used Moses' faith work in Egypt and in the wilderness to move the Jews toward the Promised Land in preparation for the coming of the Messiah.

Every person listed in Hebrews 11 had a part to play in God's big grace picture. What about believers today?

> Therefore, since we have so great a cloud of witnesses surrounding us, let us also lay aside every encumbrance and the sin which so easily entangles us, and let us run with endurance the race that is set before us, fixing our eyes on Jesus, the author and perfecter of faith, who for the joy set before Him endured the cross despising the shame, and has sat down at the right hand of the throne of God. (Heb. 12:1-2)

The faith chapter in Hebrews is not yet complete. It is still being written. Our faith work is obviously not to get Christ to Calvary and the empty tomb but to make the benefits of His work known to man. God is using us to bear fruit that is pleasing to Him. This work will be accomplished as we lay aside everything that weighs us down and the sin that so easily entangles us and run with patience the race that is before us. We are to stay on course in our race by fixing our eyes on Jesus Christ.

PAUL'S FAITH WORK

God revealed to Paul that Gentiles, former enemies of the Jews and strangers to God's plan, were to be finally included. For hundreds of years God had worked exclusively through the Jews, but He promised Abraham that in him all the nations of the earth would be blessed (Gen. 12:3). Through Paul this promise began to be realized. Paul referred to it as a mystery, the mystery of Christ.

> For this reason I, Paul, the prisoner of Jesus Christ for you Gentiles-if indeed you have heard of the dispensation of the grace of God which was given to me for you, how that by revelation He made known to me the mystery (as I wrote before in a few words, by which, when you read, you may understand my knowledge in the mystery of Christ), which in other ages was not made known to the sons of men, as it has now been revealed by the Spirit to His holy apostles and prophets. (Eph. 3:1-5)

A mystery is a truth that was previously hidden in God but is now being made known. The mystery is that both Jews and Gentiles are being placed into Christ and are becoming one new body because of the gospel. God created Paul and set him apart to preach the gospel to the Gentiles.

Paul was given grace from God in order to perform a stewardship. The word *stewardship* is very important. It is the Greek word *oikonomia*, and it is translated "dispensation." It means "household manager." At a particular time and place in history, God extended His grace to Paul, giving him the responsibility to manage the spreading of the mystery of Christ (Rom. 1:16). This was Paul's work of faith. God used him as our role model.

> It is a trustworthy statement, deserving full acceptance, that Christ Jesus came into the world to save sinners, among whom I am foremost of all. Yet for this reason I found mercy, so that in me as the foremost, Jesus Christ might demonstrate His perfect patience as an example for those who would believe in Him for eternal life. (1 Tim. 1:15-16, NASB)

The word example is translated both "pattern" and "standard." It literally means a "prototype." A prototype is a model. Paul's life and ministry is to be a model for the life and ministry of every Christian. "The ultimate sinner became the ultimate saint; God's greatest enemy became His finest servant. Somewhere within these extremes fall all the rest of us. In studying Paul's pattern, Christians can therefore learn about themselves."[11]

> The things which you learned and received and heard and saw in me, these do, and the God of peace will be with you. (Phil. 4:9)

God passed the spiritual baton from Paul to the church at Corinth. Paul preached the gospel in the ancient city of Corinth, and many

Gentiles came to faith in Jesus Christ. Paul said to the believers at Corinth, "I thank my God always concerning you for the grace of God which was given you in Christ Jesus" (1 Cor. 1:4).

Notice the change in direction of the grace coming from God. Paul did not say, "according to the grace that was given to me" but "which was given you" (Corinthian believers). God passed Paul's stewardship responsibility on to the Corinthian Christians. They, like Paul, had been given a stewardship responsibility to fulfill. Like Paul, Christians throughout history have been created, called, and saved by God to perform a faith work, a stewardship.

There are many well-meaning Christians today who see the local church as the end of ministry. Their goal is to get as many people into "church" as they possibly can. The local church is not the end of ministry. It is designed by God to be the means of ministry. The local assembly of Christians is God's equipping center for those who do His work.

Paul also carried the gospel to the Ephesians. The church at Ephesus began to grow as many came to faith in Jesus Christ. God's prescription for growth for all local churches is found right here. This passage stands as a condemnation to all of the modern market-driven techniques for growing the church. Many organizations that call themselves "church" are not using this method at all. What is God's growth prescription?

> But to each one of us grace was given according to the measure of Christ's gift. (Eph. 4:7)

Being a Christian is far more than going to Sunday school and church or listening to a sermon or singing in the choir. Every Christian is given a work of faith to accomplish within the body of Christ. We have all been equipped by God to serve.

Paul related to the Ephesians how Christ distributed gifted believers into the body of Christ.

And He Himself gave some to be apostles, some prophets,
some evangelists, and some pastors and teachers. (Eph. 4:11)

- *Apostles* included Paul and others sent with God's message.
- *Prophets* were those who preached the message of God.
- *Evangelists* are those who are gifted to share the gospel.
- *Pastors* are those who shepherd the flock of God.
- *Teachers* are those gifted to teach the children of God.

It was not Paul's desire to mention *all* the gifted people here.
Paul's goal was to show *why* these gifted people are distributed
throughout the body. Here is God's plan for building His church
(Matt. 16:18). He gave no other plan! We have all been equipped
by God and strategically placed into the body of Christ in every
generation for two reasons.

For the equipping of the saints for the work of ministry, for
the edifying of the body of Christ. (Eph. 4:12)

- For the equipping of the saints for the work of ministry

The word *equipping* means "to train or to prepare." The local
church is a spiritual training center. As amazing as this may sound,
the Bible never instructs an unbeliever to attend church. The local
church is designed to train Christians. There are many passages that
instruct the church to take the gospel into the world. Believers are
then to be brought into the local assembly to be taught and trained.

Bible colleges and seminaries have been used of God in significant
ways. It is God's design, however, that every believer be trained to
do the work of ministry within the confines of the local church.
Believers are taught to perform this work of ministry.

Work is the Greek word *ergon*. It implies energy being used.
Ministry is the word *diakinos*. It means "to serve." Paul was not
speaking specifically of elders, pastors, or deacons but of the special

service of every member of the body. Every Christian has a work of faith to do, and they are to be trained in the local church to do it.

- For the edifying of the body of Christ

Here is the ultimate goal of God's stewards. *Edifying* is a combination word made up of *oiko,* "to build," and *dome,* the "top or roof." Together the word means "building from the ground floor all the way to the top." We are all to grow to spiritual maturity.

Spiritual maturity is to be measured against the stature of the fullness of Christ. The characteristics of our lives are to reflect the characteristics of His life to the world. How will we know when this has been achieved?

> That we should no longer be children, tossed to and fro and carried about with every wind of doctrine, by the trickery of men, in the cunning craftiness of deceitful plotting, but, speaking the truth in love, may grow up in all things into Him who is the head—Christ–from whom the whole body, joined and knit together by what every joint supplies, according to the effective working by which every part does its share, causes growth of the body for the edifying of itself in love. (Eph. 4:14-16)

When believers reach a mature status, they will no longer be like little children, confused and sidetracked by the false teaching of deceivers who seek to destroy. Instead, they will speak the truth in love and will grow up in all things into Him who is our head, even Christ.

It is from our head–the Lord Jesus Christ–that the whole body fits together! Even though He is seated at the right hand of the Father in heaven, His life and ministry to the world continues to be communicated through every part of His body (Heb. 1:3; 1:13; 8:1; 10:12; 12:2).

How do we discover our gifts? As we serve the Lord and observe and receive the gifts from others in the body, our own gifts begin to become clear.

If our gift is Bible teaching, we are to teach other believers the word of God. As we are taught by others and observe their gift, God will impress upon us the desire to teach.

If our gift is mercy, we will show mercy to those who need it. If mercy is our gift, we will be challenged to use it as we observe this gift in others.

If our gift is helps, we are to help with all the tasks of the church, and in doing so we will teach others how to help the body of Christ and encourage others with the same gift to become involved

If our gift is faith, we use our giftedness to trust God to do what He says He will do and to train others to live by faith.

If our gift is administration, we organize the church in a godly way and train others in the proper way to administer the activities of the church.

If our gift is evangelism, we share the gospel with the lost and teach other believers how to share the message of the gospel and motivate them to do so.

If our work of ministry is encouragement, we are to encourage others and by doing so we teach others how to encourage.

The church will grow both numerically and spiritually in direct proportion to the quality of the work of gifted believers. This should shout to us as God's prescription for the spiritual growth of the church. Missing is the exclusive role of a pastor to equip the flock. Paul does not mention human schemes, programs, or motivational methods.

Every member of the body of Christ is to grow based upon the spiritual contribution of every other member in the body. Every believer has been uniquely gifted of God to play a part. What is to be achieved when every believer performs his stewardship?

> Till we all come to the unity of the faith and of the
> knowledge of the Son of God, to a perfect man, to the
> measure of the stature of the fullness of Christ. (Eph. 4:13)

Every Christian is to come to understand what it means to live by faith within the community of believers (2 Cor. 5:7). Every Christian is also to have an adequate knowledge of the Son of God, His deity, His life, His death, His resurrection, His ascension, and His present ministry. Every Christian is to become spiritually mature and productive.

The body of Christ is alive and well on the earth. Jesus Christ continues His ministry to His body through His body. His body grows–spiritually and numerically–as a direct result of the ministry that every believer performs. When every part does its share, the body matures and grows in love. That is the purpose of every believer's faith work.

In fact, it is the ministry of each believer that knits the body together. This is God's prescription for growth in the local church. In every generation since Pentecost, God continues to build the body of Christ exactly the same way. There is no other method of church growth taught in the Bible. It is painfully clear how far we have strayed from this formula today.

PETER'S TESTIMONY

Peter's letter was written at a time when the body of Christ was under great persecution from the emperors in Rome. The recipients of 1 Peter received word that the Roman authorities had discovered where believers were located and had possibly sent soldiers to arrest them. They felt their time on earth was short.

Peter's encouragement to them was extremely important! Notice what Peter considered to be the most important activity this church could be involved in during this critical time for them.

But the end of all things is at hand; therefore be serious and watchful in your prayers. And above all things have fervent love for one another, for love will cover a multitude of sins. Be hospitable to one another without grumbling. As each one has received a gift, minister it to one another, as good stewards of the manifold grace of God. If anyone speaks, let him speak as the oracles of God. If anyone ministers, let him do it as with the ability which God supplies, that in all things God may be glorified through Jesus Christ, to whom belong the glory and the dominion forever and ever. Amen. (1 Pet. 4:7-11)

Peter could have instructed this church to do many things, but he chose the areas of ministry that he felt to be the most important. He charged them first of all to pray. Prayer is not optional for Christians. Peter then mentioned love for one another. It is a good thing to stir up love in the body.

Notice carefully what Peter said last. The believers were to be busy ministering their gifts to one another. He encouraged them to serve each other as good stewards of God's magnificent grace. How could God make it any clearer?

Jesus Christ is the beginning and end of our faith (Rom. 1:16-17). He created us, set us apart, called us to Himself, and equipped us to fulfill a divine destiny. He will finish in each of us what He starts (Phil. 1:6).

CHAPTER 9

A GLIMPSE OF THE CHRISTIAN'S EDUCATION

> Blessed *is* the man who trusts in the LORD, and whose hope is the LORD. For he shall be like a tree planted by the waters, which spreads out its roots by the river, and will not fear when heat comes; but its leaf will be green, and will not be anxious in the year of drought, nor will cease from yielding fruit. (Jer. 17:7-8)

In order to accomplish our work of faith, we must be taught God's Word. Christians are born again into God's forever family as spiritual babies. Like a young tree planted by the rivers of water, it is God's will that we grow and mature and produce fruit. Peter spelled out the main ingredient for growth.

> Like newborn babies, long for the pure milk of the word, so that by it you may grow in respect to salvation. (1 Pet. 2:2, NASB)

Newborn babies come into the world with the instinctive desire to take in milk because without it they cannot grow. The word *desire* means "to have a deep continuous longing for." Christians must have this same hunger to grow spiritually and must take in God's word in order to satisfy their hunger. There is no other method for growth in the Bible.

> It is written, "Man shall not live by bread alone but by every word that proceeds from the mouth of God." (Matt. 4:4)

Every word in the Bible is placed there by God for this purpose.

> All Scripture is given by inspiration of God, and is profitable for doctrine, for reproof, for correction, for instruction in righteousness, that the man of God may be complete, thoroughly equipped for every good work. (2 Tim. 3:16-17)

The word *inspiration* means "God breathed." Every word in the Bible comes from the breath of God. As a result:

- Scripture is profitable for doctrine. *Doctrine* means "truth or divine instruction." Scripture has the ability to teach us God's truth.
- Scripture is profitable for reproof. It not only has the capability to teach us God's truth, but it stands against that which God says is not true.
- Scripture is profitable for correction. The word *correction* means to "restore something to its original condition." Scripture is God's plumb line to reestablish His truth.
- Scripture is profitable for instruction in righteousness. The Bible has the ability to train Christians to do what is right.

The result is that the man of God may be spiritually complete, thoroughly equipped for every good work that God calls us to do.

STUDY METICULOUSLY

We are to carefully study the Bible in order to comprehend what it teaches. Paul instructed Timothy, his young son in the faith:

> Be diligent to present yourself approved to God, a worker
> who does not need to be ashamed, rightly dividing the
> word of truth. (2 Tim. 2:14-15)

Diligent is a synonym for "hard work." There is no shortcut to
a Bible education. Diligence is giving one's all, a maximum effort.
Bible study involves spending hour after hour pouring oneself into
the text, breaking it down into its smallest parts, attempting to
understand every detail.

Bible study goes far beyond just reading the text or searching for
specific passages or small nuggets from which one can put together
a sermon or a Bible lesson and it is a long way from quickly glancing
through the text. Bible study is a careful word-by-word, line-by-
line, verse-by-verse, paragraph-by-paragraph study. It is seeking to
discover in the proper context the precise meaning that the writer
was teaching.

We are to be careful not to read into the text our own human ideas
or opinions. We dare not twist the text to make it say what we would
like for it to say. This is called *isogesis,* or reading into the text our
own bias. Many people do this to accommodate their own opinions.
This is why many people respond, "Well, that's your interpretation."
Since the Holy Spirit penned the book and that same Spirit lives
in each believer, then each believer should come up with the same
interpretation.

Why must we study the Bible verse-by-verse and word-by-
word? Because this is the way God has brought it down to us. I have
personally found that it is wise to stay away from commentaries or
other Bible study sources until I have exhausted myself in a thorough
observation and study of the text.

The purpose for this diligent form of study, according to Paul,
is threefold. First is that this method will meet God's approval. The
word *approved* means "approved by testing and found worthy." God
is looking over my shoulder as I study. He is there in the moment.
My desire is not to please men but to please Him.

The second reason for diligent Bible study is so that I will not be ashamed. I will stand before God and give an account to Him of how I have handled His Word. I will not be ashamed when I face Him if I have done an adequate job.

And finally, I am to be diligent in my study so I can rightly divide the Word. Literally it says "handling accurately the word of truth." This short phrase translates a participle that means to cut straight. It was used of a craftsman cutting a straight line, of a farmer plowing a straight furrow, of a mason setting a straight line of bricks, or of workmen building a straight road.[12] I am to strive for accuracy in my study and my teaching.

Catch this glimpse! There are three different people groups on this planet. Paul instructs us to give no offense, either to the Jews or to the Greeks (the Gentiles) or to the church of God (1 Cor. 10:32). The Jews are different from Gentiles, and the Jews and Gentiles are different from the church of Jesus Christ. The word of God is written *for* all of us. However, portions are not written specifically *to* us. For instance, the message of the gospel is designed for all people, both Jew and Gentile! Once a Jew or Gentile has come to faith in Jesus Christ, he becomes a Christian.

There are portions of the Old Testament written specifically to Jews. Exodus tells the Jews that they are not to boil a young goat in its mother's milk (Ex. 23:19). That is obviously not written to Christians.

There are portions of the Bible written to Christians to teach us who we are and how we are to live. Unsaved Jews and Gentiles are not instructed to live the Christian life in order to be saved. As a student, I am to be able to discern what portions of the Bible are written to whom and why. I am to learn to rightly divide the Word of God.

As a result, I become a mature believer and ultimately produce fruit that is pleasing to God. In the process, I am weaned off milk, the elementary principles in the Word, and move on to solid food, the deeper truths of Bible doctrine.

A sad truth today is that many have been exposed to the Bible for years but have never sufficiently matured in their faith. They have been given time and adequate resources to grow, but they have not. This was true even in Paul's day.

> I fed you with milk and not with solid food; for until now you were not able to receive it, and even now you are still not able. (1 Cor. 3:2)

The writer of Hebrews said:

> For everyone who partakes *only* of milk *is* unskilled in the word of righteousness, for he is a babe. But solid food belongs to those who are of full age, *that is,* those who by reason of use have their senses exercised to discern both good and evil. (Heb. 5:13-14)

We are to diligently study the Bible.

MEMORIZE CONSISTENTLY

Another important aspect of Bible study is scripture memorization.

> Your word I have hidden in my heart that I might not sin against You. (Ps. 119:11)

The single most important thing that has been used in my life to give me the amazing glimpses of God's grace that I have received is Bible memorization. I have spent much time memorizing God's Word. There is no more effective way to allow the Spirit of God to teach you than to flood your mind with His Word. I have included at the end of this book a method of memorizing the text and a list of verses to memorize. The key to success is to be faithful to do it year after year.

MEDITATE CONSTANTLY

The third means the Holy Spirit uses to teach us God's word is meditation. *Meditation* is "to think about carefully and at length, consider, contemplate, deliberate, muse, ponder, reflect, think over, think through, turn over, or weigh."

> This Book of the Law shall not depart from your mouth, but you shall meditate in it day and night, that you may observe to do according to all that is written in it. For then you will make your way prosperous, and then you will have good success. (Josh. 1:8)

Hebrew is a picture language. The words are formed from pictures so what one ends up with is a word picture. The Hebrew word *meditate* is to muse. It could be like a cow chewing its cud. It is very similar to the act of rumination.

A friend of mine used this illustration on a mission trip we made to India. He was teaching Indian pastors the importance of meditating on Scripture. They did not seem to be tuned in. Suddenly it hit him. A beautiful illustration of this truth was all around them. The Brahman cows were everywhere, and they were all busy chewing their cud.

Rumination is the process a cow uses to chew cud. The cow has several stomachs. She can chew her cud and then swallow it into one of her lower stomachs. When she desires, she can pull the cud back into her mouth and continue to chew on it.

This is exactly what we are to do with God's Word. We are to study it, memorize it, and then meditate on it. When we are alone, we are to pull it back into our minds and ponder it again and again. The Indian pastors got it!

How long are we to meditate on the Word? We are to meditate on the word of God day and night our entire lives.

> Meditate on these things; give yourself entirely to them, that your progress may be evident to all. Take heed to

yourself and to the doctrine. Continue in them, for in doing this you will save both yourself and those who hear you. (1 Tim. 4:15-16)

Learning the word of God involves the hard work of meticulously studying it, memorizing it, and meditating on it.

THE SPIRIT'S TEACHING

How are Christians actually taught God's Word? It is the job of the Holy Spirit to teach us.

I still have many things to say to you, but you cannot bear them now. However, when He, the Spirit of truth, has come, He will guide you into all truth; for He will not speak on His own authority, but whatever He hears He will speak; and He will tell you things to come. He will glorify Me, for He will take of what is Mine and declare it to you. All things that the Father has are Mine. Therefore I said that He will take of Mine and declare it to you. (Jn. 16:12-15)

Jesus had been regularly teaching His disciples, yet He had much more to say. The men, however, did not have the spiritual capacity to understand His words and time was running out. Jesus promised that He would send them another teacher, the Holy Spirit, and that His purpose would be to guide them into all truth. The Holy Spirit would not speak from the platform of His own authority but would teach the things that Christ wanted taught.

Paul gave tremendous insight into how the Spirit teaches us. His letter to the Corinthian church reminded them of his one goal of preaching the gospel to them.

For Christ did not send me to baptize, but to preach the gospel, not with wisdom of words, lest the cross of Christ should be made of no effect. (1 Cor. 1:17)

The Corinthian believers were divided over the tendency to follow human leaders and not Jesus Christ. Some were partial to Paul because he had baptized them. Others favored Apollos or Peter. Paul emphasized that Christ did not send him to baptize, but to preach the gospel. He was teaching the Corinthians that they were majoring on minor things. Preaching the gospel was priority. The gospel is the truth concerning the identity, death, and resurrection of Jesus Christ (1 Cor. 15:1-3). That is the major truth–not baptism.

Paul reminded them that he did not preach the gospel to them by using the wisdom of human words. To have done this would have mixed human wisdom with God's gospel, and thus nullified the effect of the gospel. The cross work of Jesus Christ is effective only when it is preached clearly.

> For the message of the cross is foolishness to those who are perishing, but to us who are being saved it is the power of God. (1 Cor. 1:18)

When the gospel is taught clearly, it is either considered foolish or powerful depending on who is listening. To those who are on their way to hell, it appears to be foolish. To those of us who are being saved, it is the sweetest message on the planet, the very power of God. Paul quickly added these words from Isaiah:

> For it is written: "I will destroy the wisdom of the wise, and bring to nothing the understanding of the prudent." (1 Cor. 1:19; see Isa. 29:14)

God seems to delight in baffling the wisdom of man. He will ultimately destroy all human wisdom and render human understanding of no consequence.

Paul then compared human wisdom with God's wisdom.

> Where is the wise? Where is the scribe? Where is the
> disputer of this age? Has not God made foolish the wisdom
> of this world? (1 Cor. 1:20)

Worldly wisdom can never accomplish God's will. The wisdom
of man will never make this world a better place. At the end of man's
greatest achievements, there will still be war and hunger and disease
and corruption of every kind. The world charted by man's wisdom
will never lead to peace on earth and good will toward man, despite
what the politicians say.

Human wisdom cannot be used to lead a spiritually dead person to
knowledge of the living God. It pleases God through the foolishness
of the message preached to save those who believe (1 Cor. 1:21). God
has chosen to use what the world considers to be a foolish message to
save those who believe it. The message of God's saving grace is not
foolishness, but God uses that which appears to be foolish to save.

- The fact that all men died spiritually in Adam appears to the
  human mind to be foolish.
- The fact that Adam's sin is passed down to every generation
  of man appears to the human mind to be foolish.
- The fact that God became flesh through the virgin birth
  appears to the human mind to be foolish.
- The fact that God in the person of Christ died on the cross
  in order to pay for man's sin appears to the human mind to
  be foolish.
- The fact that Jesus Christ rose from the dead appears to the
  human mind to be foolish.
- The fact that God gives eternal life to those who believe these
  facts and trust in Jesus Christ appears to the human mind to
  be foolish.

This is the very truth that God uses to give life to those who
believe. Paul invited the Corinthians to take a look around at the
fellow believers sitting next to them.

> For you see your calling, brethren, that not many wise according to the flesh, not many mighty, not many noble, are called. But God has chosen the foolish things of the world to put to shame the wise, and God has chosen the weak things of the world to put to shame the things which are mighty; and the base things of the world and the things which are despised God has chosen, and the things which are not, to bring to nothing the things that are, that no flesh should glory in His presence. But of Him you are in Christ Jesus, who became for us wisdom from God—and righteousness and sanctification and redemption—that, as it is written, "He who glories, let him glory in the LORD. (1 Cor. 1:26-31)

It should be obvious that those sitting among the Corinthian believers had not received the new birth through their superior intellect or strength or status. Evidently those endowed with superior human wisdom were in short supply in the church there.

So if the gospel is not to be preached or received through human means, how does the gospel work? Paul said, "But of Him you are in Christ Jesus." *Of Him* is a genitive of source. All of these people became Christians from the source of God. God alone must make it happen. In order to do so, God uses the simple gospel message.

God has never been impressed with human greatness. When Jesus came to earth, He could have come to any one of the world's great capital cities. He chose instead to enter the world in a little village called Bethlehem, and He chose to be born in a stable to a lowly peasant girl. When He was ready to call His disciples, rather than going to the religious elite, it appeared that He went to the very ones that the world had rejected, the tax collectors, prostitutes, and those whom everyone called sinners (Matt. 11:19).

In fact, according to Jesus Christ, the greatest man who ever lived was John the Baptist. Jesus said, "Truly I say to you, among those born of women there has not arisen anyone greater than John the Baptist" (Matt. 11:11).

What do we know about John? "He had no formal education, no special family pedigree, no training in a trade or profession, no money, no military rank, no political position, no social standing, no reputation, no impressive appearance or special talent. He came out of the desert wearing camel's hair, a leather belt, and had been living on a diet of locust and wild honey. John the Baptist fit none of the world's requirements for greatness but all of God's."[13]

When Paul came to the Corinthian people, he did not come with excellence of speech but he came declaring the testimony of God. He simply taught the gospel. He was determined that he would know nothing except Jesus Christ and Him crucified. His speech and his preaching were not with persuasive words of man's wisdom but a demonstration of the Spirit and of power (1 Cor. 2:1-4).

Paul had no desire to bring attention to himself at all. He did not attempt to use logic to convince the Corinthians that what he said about Jesus Christ was true. He did not seek to compete with the world in order to market the gospel. He depended solely upon the Spirit of God and the powerful seed of the word of God to accomplish God's purpose.

More than anything, Paul desired that the faith that his hearers placed in Christ would not be the result of the wisdom of men but of the power of God (1 Cor. 2:5). Their conversion would be a legitimate work of God and not some emotional decision based on the strength of his words.

Human logic and rationalism can be very powerful and very persuasive. A lawyer must be skilled in debater's technique. Two lawyers represent their clients. One is guilty; the other is not. It really is of little consequence what the truth is. What matters is what the jury believes. What the jury believes is that which the lawyers want them to believe. The lawyer who can make the most convincing case can win.

Paul realized that he could not use such techniques in order to make the gospel work. He could not mix philosophy with the gospel and still have the gospel. He made the conscious decision that the heart of his message was the Christ who was crucified and raised and that the message would be given in simple understandable words (1 Cor. 2:2; 2 Cor. 11:3). The result, therefore, was solely in the hands of God.

This is the wisdom taught by the Spirit of God. Paul said, "We speak wisdom among those who are mature, yet not the wisdom of this age, nor of the rulers of this age, who are coming to nothing" (1 Cor. 2:6). The people who believed Paul are referred to as the mature, or the spiritual people (1 Cor. 2:13, 15).

Many may be moved emotionally and respond tearfully to touching stories and heartrending music which are laced with scripture passages. The stories may be filled with illustrations of shared love or with drama and compassion, and they all may be wrapped around the name Jesus. Those making decisions may have rested their hope on the wisdom of men and not the power of God.

Paul wrote in contrast:

> But we speak the wisdom of God in a mystery, the hidden wisdom which God ordained before the ages for our glory, which none of the rulers of this age knew; for had they known, they would not have crucified the Lord of glory. (1 Cor. 2:7-9)

The rulers of Paul's time obviously did not understand God's wisdom, because had they known it they would not have carried out the crucifixion. In contrast, Paul said that God's wisdom is a mysterious wisdom—a hidden wisdom—that God predestined before the ages of time for our glory.

God's wisdom does not come from the human realm. In fact, Paul wrote this amazing truth.

> But as it is written: "Eye has not seen, nor ear heard, nor have entered into the heart of man the things which

God has prepared for those who love Him." But God has revealed them to us through His Spirit." (1 Cor. 2:10)

God's wisdom is not that which human eyes have seen. It does not come through seeing mystical visions or through hearing strange voices. And God's wisdom is not rehashed human thoughts, ideas, or opinions. God's wisdom is that which has never before entered the mind of man. That is an awesome thought!

How do we receive this wisdom? There is only one way!

> For what man knows the things of a man except the spirit of the man which is in him? Even so no one knows the things of God except the Spirit of God. Now we have received, not the spirit of the world, but the Spirit who is from God, that we might know the things that have been freely given to us by God. These things we also speak, not in words which man's wisdom teaches but which the Holy Spirit teaches, comparing spiritual things with spiritual. (1 Cor. 2:11-13)

This passage contains a wealth of spiritual knowledge. A man knows only his own secret thoughts, not those of another. Likewise, no one knows the thoughts of God except the Spirit of God. Since we have received the Spirit of God, we can know the things freely given to us by God.

Catch this incredible glimpse! God reveals to us truths that human eyes have never seen before and human ears have never heard before, and truths that have never entered the mind of any human being before.

I am fascinated with the little phrase "comparing spiritual things with spiritual."

This means that as I am diligent to study the word of God, every word, every line, every paragraph, God the Holy Spirit begins to teach my human spirit the things of the Spirit of God. As I study the words of the Bible, the Spirit places thoughts in my mind, allowing me to see with my mind's eye God's amazing plan for this world. This is God's method of teaching every believer His wisdom, His mind. It is not different insights for different believers, but it is the same truth using the same method.

The Christian cannot approach the text looking for or seeking to find these divine truths. God does not give them to us this way. He gives them to those who diligently study the word of God line by line, hour after hour. God opens His wisdom to those who have a sincere desire to know Him through His Word. He gives His wisdom to those who hunger and thirst for it and work hard to get it.

God has not taught me everything that I desired to know about any given subject in His Word. He has probably taught others much more. He has given me just small "glimpses" of His plan. A *glimpse* is a "brief, incomplete view or look, a brief flash of light." But as I began to connect these small glimpses one with the other, God's magnificent wisdom began to emerge–the eternal nature of Jesus Christ, why God took on flesh, the truth concerning the virgin birth, the fact surrounding the death of Christ, His resurrection, His ascension back into heaven, the truth that God has provided His salvation by grace alone, through faith alone, in Jesus Christ alone–to name just a few.

We were visiting some friends in Houston, Texas, some years ago. My children brought home from a trip to the mall a hologram. Holograms are pictures hidden within a picture. They handed me the print of a beautiful American flag and asked me to find the hidden picture. I tried and tried, but I just could not see it!

My daughter kept repeating, "Dad, just look deep within the flag." I tried time and again. Finally, after many attempts I caught a glimpse of something! Ah, there it was. Hidden in the flag was a beautiful eagle with its wings spread majestically. *That's fascinating,* I thought.

The hologram is a perfect illustration of the Holy Spirit opening the truth of God's word to the mind of the student. Glimpses of grace come only as God the Holy Spirit reveals them to us. It has been these glimpses that the Spirit of God has used to teach me and to motivate me through the years. Day by day, year by year, more of God's magnificent wisdom begins to emerge just like the eagle in the hologram.

CHAPTER 10

A GLIMPSE OF THE CHRISTIAN'S ASSEMBLY

The true church of Jesus Christ is not an organization, as we have already discovered. It is a living organism made up of regenerated people. However, this spiritual group is instructed by God to meet together on a regular basis.

> Let us hold fast the confession of our hope without wavering, for He who promised is faithful. And let us consider one another in order to stir up love and good works, not forsaking the assembling of ourselves together, as is the manner of some, but exhorting one another, and so much the more as you see the Day approaching. (Heb. 10:23-25)

This local assembly is "the church." Again, the church is not to be confused with the building that houses the church. The church is the people meeting inside the building. The local church consists of baptized Christians meeting together for Bible study, prayer, the Lord's Supper, baptisms, fellowship, and to fulfill their stewardship responsibilities.

Speaking of the early church meetings, we read:

> And they continued steadfastly in the apostles' doctrine
> and fellowship, in the breaking of bread, and in prayers.
> (Acts 2:42)

The *apostles' doctrine* was the first portions of the compiled
written word of God taught to the church. These documents, no
doubt, included the Old Testament, many of the words of Christ, as
well as words from the apostles.

The word *fellowship* means "to have all things in common." This
common fellowship is the glue that holds Christians together. We are
joined together by common doctrinal beliefs such as the inerrancy of
the Bible, the gospel of grace, the deity of Christ, and so on. We share
the common goals of giving the gospel to the lost and equipping each
other to serve our Lord. We are to be faithful in meeting together.

MEETING ON SUNDAY

Why does the local church meet on Sunday? It all began with this
Old Testament passage.

> Thus the heavens and the earth were completed, and all
> their hosts. By the seventh day God completed His work
> which He had done, and He rested on the seventh day from
> all His work which He had done. Then God blessed the
> seventh day and sanctified it, because in it He rested from
> all His work which God had created and made. (Gen. 2:1-3)

By the seventh day of creation God had completed His work.
According to our calendar, the seventh day is Saturday. God rested
on Saturday. If someone rests it usually means that they are tired,
but God does not tire. *Rested* is a translation of the Hebrew word
shaboth (pronounced *Shabat*). It is from this word that we get our
English transliteration *Sabbath*. The word could better be translated
"to cease."

> While the earth remains, seedtime and harvest, cold and
> heat, winter and summer, and day and night shall not cease
> *(shaboth).* (Gen. 8:22)

Why did God cease His creative work? His creative plan was complete! God had created everything that needed to be made in seven literal days. There was nothing left to do. He had made everything necessary for man's existence. God was fully satisfied with what He had done. He deemed that nothing else had to be added or taken away to please Him.

> Then God blessed the seventh day and sanctified it,
> because in it He rested from all His work which God had
> created and made. (Gen. 1:3)

This Sabbath rest became very important to the Jew. It was to be set apart as a memorial that God had done everything necessary to preserve them and provide for them. The Jews were to do no work on that day. The Sabbath was so important that God included the observance of the Sabbath in the Ten Commandments (Ex. 20:8-11). The Jews honored the Sabbath for hundreds of years.

Catch this glimpse! It was not mere chance that Jesus Christ died during a Sabbath festival (Jn. 19:31). He fulfilled God's Sabbath. By His death, He provided everything necessary for salvation. Man is to cease all human effort to please God in order to be saved and trust in the Lord Jesus Christ by faith (Eph. 2:8-9; Titus 3:5; Rom. 4:5).

What about the church and its meeting time? Is the church to meet on the Sabbath? The resurrection of Jesus Christ took place on the first day of the week, which is Sunday (Mark 16:9). The event was so awesome, so life changing, that it motivated the disciples to stop meeting on the Sabbath and to begin to meet on the first day of the week (Acts 20:7).

This marks the impact that the resurrection made on the Jews. The church of Jesus Christ has continued throughout history to meet on the first day of the week. Since Jesus Christ fulfilled the Sabbath, there is no command in the New Testament for Christians to observe the Sabbath.

> So let no one judge you in food or in drink, or regarding a festival or a new moon or sabbaths, which are a shadow of things to come, but the substance is of Christ. (Col. 2:16-17)

God gave the church only two ordinances: water baptism and the Lord's Supper. An ordinance is a picture or a symbol that publicly acknowledges a spiritual reality. The ordinances represent the two most significant events in the life of the Christian. Water baptism is a picture of our entrance into the family of God. The Lord's Supper pictures our personal fellowship with Jesus Christ.

WATER BAPTISM

Before His departure back into heaven, the Lord gave what is called "the Great Commission." He commanded His disciples to make other disciples.

> Go therefore and make disciples of all the nations, baptizing them in the name of the Father and the Son and the Holy Spirit. (Matt. 28:19)

The commands to go, make disciples, and baptize are not optional; they are essential. Through water baptism new believers make their invisible faith in Christ visible. The New Testament way of identifying new Christians is not the raising of hands or walking aisles, or even filling out cards. The New Testament method of identifying new Christians is water baptism (Acts 2:41).

It would be similar to showing a friend a picture of my new granddaughter. The picture is not my granddaughter; it is just a picture. The moment that we trust Christ as Savior, we are immersed into His body; we are identified with His death and His resurrection (Rom. 6:3). This is an invisible but real event.

When we are water baptized, we show a picture of this truth. When we are immersed into the water, we illustrate our being immersed into Christ's death. When we come out of the water, we signify that we have been raised to new life in Him (Rom. 6:4).

By water baptism we publicly share the good news of Jesus Christ with others without saying a word. By this symbol, we are challenged to walk in our new resurrected life (Acts 8:12-13; Acts 9:18; Acts 10:47; Acts 19:5). People who attend a believer's public baptism actually "see" the gospel.

THE LORD'S SUPPER

What is the purpose of the Lord's Supper? Paul explained in his letter to the church at Corinth.

> For I received from the Lord that which I also delivered to you: that the Lord Jesus on the same night in which He was betrayed took bread; and when He had given thanks, He broke it and said, "Take, eat; this is My body which is broken for you; do this in remembrance of Me." In the same manner He also took the cup after supper, saying, "This cup is the new covenant in My blood. This do, as often as you drink it, in remembrance of Me." For as often as you eat this bread and drink this cup, you proclaim the Lord's death till He comes. (1 Cor. 11:23-26)

The sacrificial death of many animals in Old Testament times confirmed the old covenant repeatedly, but the blood of Jesus Christ ratified the new covenant once for all (Heb. 9:28). It is new in that it is the saving covenant to which all the Old Testament shadows pointed (Heb. 10:1-6). The new deliverance is from sin to salvation, from death to life, from Satan's realm to God's kingdom.

The Jews celebrated the old covenant by sharing the Passover meal together. Following the death and resurrection of Christ, the Lord's Supper replaced the Jewish Passover. We now eat the bread and drink the cup, not to remember the Red Sea and the Exodus but to remember the cross and the Savior.

At the last supper in the upper room, Christ said simply, "Do this in remembrance of Me." It is a command from the lips of our Lord himself. Therefore, sharing in the Lord's Supper is not optional for believers. We are to have communion on a regular basis if we are to be faithful to the Lord. The Lord's Supper is God's method of jogging the memory of believers concerning the life and death of Jesus Christ. The bread symbolizes His perfect body that was broken for us. The wine symbolizes His blood that was shed for the remission of our sin. The supper reveals the facts of the gospel.

We are to observe the Lord's Supper until He comes, so it serves to remind us that He is coming again (1 Cor. 11:26). The Supper also reminds us that we are a unified body, Christ's body, even His church.

The Corinthian church was abusing the Lord's Supper. They had turned it into a drunken party. Paul wrote:

> Therefore when you come together in one place, it is not to eat the Lord's Supper. For in eating, each one takes his own supper ahead of others; and one is hungry and another is drunk. What! Do you not have houses to eat and drink in? Or do you despise the church of God and shame those who have nothing? What shall I say to you? Shall I praise you in this? I do not praise you. (1 Cor. 11:20-22)

The wealthy were arriving early and eating their food without sharing it with others. The poor who arrived later with their food to share were left with only what they had brought. The first comers had eaten and had begun to drink. By the time the whole group got there, some were already drunk. When it was time to share the Lord's Supper, all were out of fellowship with Jesus Christ. Paul continued:

> Therefore whoever eats this bread or drinks this cup of the Lord in an unworthy manner will be guilty of the body and blood of the Lord. But let a man examine himself, and

so let him eat of the bread and drink of the cup. For he who eats and drinks in an unworthy manner eats and drinks judgment to himself, not discerning the Lord's body. For this reason many are weak and sick among you, and many sleep. For if we would judge ourselves, we would not be judged. But when we are judged, we are chastened by the Lord, that we may not be condemned with the world. Therefore, my brethren, when you come together to eat, wait for one another. But if anyone is hungry, let him eat at home, lest you come together for judgment. And the rest I will set in order when I come. (1 Cor. 11:27-34)

The Lord's Supper is designed by God to remind us that we are to fellowship with the person of Jesus Christ. He is always to be considered our special guest at the meal. If we are out of fellowship, we are to allow the Holy Spirit to reveal our sin to us and we are to confess that sin and be restored to fellowship. We should always leave the meal in fellowship with Christ and with each other. If we do not, we are set to receive discipline from God.

CHRISTIAN GIVING

What is to be the Christian's position on giving money to the church? The ministry of giving is a special act of worship expected of every Christian. Are Christians supposed to tithe?

You shall truly tithe all the increase of your grain that the field produces year by year. And you shall eat before the LORD your God, in the place where He chooses to make His name abide, the tithe of your grain and your new wine and your oil, of the firstborn of your herds and your flocks, that you may learn to fear the LORD your God always. (Deut. 14:22-23)

At the end of every third year you shall bring out the tithe of your produce of that year and store it up within your gates. And the Levite, because he has no portion nor

> inheritance with you, and the stranger and the fatherless
> and the widow who are within your gates, may come and
> eat and be satisfied, that the LORD your God may bless you
> in all the work of your hand which you do. (Deut. 14:28-29)

Dr. Arnold Fruchtenbaum has the best view on tithing under law that I have read. I quote him here.

- First of all, the actual Mosaic tithe was not 10 percent but 22-23 percent. That is because there were two annual tithes of 10 percent each and a third tithe every third year. The total averages out to 22-23 percent.
- Second, the tithing itself was aimed strictly at the farming community, which most Jews were members of. They had to tithe from what was grown and what was raised such as flocks. Anyone else outside the field of farming would simply pay the annual half shekel at Passover.
- Third, tithing was part of the Mosaic Law and therefore was only in force as long as the Mosaic Law was in force.
- Fourth, the biblical principle for today's giving is not based upon tithing but based upon giving as the Lord has prospered. From week to week the percentile might be different depending on the obligations we might have. The Mosaic Law came to an end when Messiah died on the cross.
- Fifth, the Bible nowhere says we are to give our entire offering to the local church. The verses used to show that the church is to tithe are verses that deal with the Mosaic Law. The storehouse (Malachi 3:10) was in the temple compound where the food was stored and not the church treasury of today. Law giving was not voluntary at all. It was marked by the words "you will." God levied this giving as a tax.[14]

Within God's plan of grace, He changed the pattern for giving. Paul penned God's new plan in 2 Corinthians 8-9. Many early believers–especially Jewish–found themselves ostracized from the rest of society. They were social outcasts and unable to find work. They became destitute and at the mercy of the world. Paul saw the necessity of raising money for these believers. When he did so, he gave us some important truth concerning grace giving.

> Moreover, brethren, we make known to you the grace of God bestowed on the churches of Macedonia: that in a great trial of affliction the abundance of their joy and their deep poverty abounded in the riches of their liberality. For I bear witness that according to their ability, yes, and beyond their ability, they were freely willing, imploring us with much urgency that we would receive the gift and the fellowship of the ministering to the saints. And not only as we had hoped, but they first gave themselves to the Lord, and then to us by the will of God. So we urged Titus, that as he had begun, so he would also complete this grace in you as well. (2 Cor. 8:1-6)

The Macedonian believers gave sacrificially and liberally even out of their own poverty. They gave first of themselves and then of their means.

> Therefore I thought it necessary to exhort the brethren to go to you ahead of time, and prepare your generous gift beforehand, which you had previously promised, that it may be ready as a matter of generosity and not as a grudging obligation. (2 Cor. 9:1-5)

The Corinthian believers prepared the gift beforehand and laid it aside. Paul encouraged them to give generously and not grudgingly.

> But this I say: He who sows sparingly will also reap sparingly, and he who sows bountifully will also reap bountifully. So let each one give as he purposes in his heart, not grudgingly or of necessity; for God loves a cheerful giver. And God is able to make all grace abound

toward you, that you, always having all sufficiency in all things, may have abundance for every good work. As it is written: He has dispersed abroad, He has given to the poor; His righteousness endures forever. Now may He who supplies seed to the sower, and bread for food, supply and multiply the seed you have sown and increase the fruits of your righteousness, while you are enriched in everything for all liberality, which causes thanksgiving through us to God. For the administration of this service not only supplies the needs of the saints, but also is abounding through many thanksgivings to God, while, through the proof of this ministry, they glorify God for the obedience of your confession to the gospel of Christ, and for your liberal sharing with them and all men, and by their prayer for you, who long for you because of the exceeding grace of God in you. Thanks be to God for His indescribable gift! (2 Cor. 9:6-15)

Grace giving promotes generosity. When believers have first given themselves to the Lord, they realize that everything they have comes from Him and belongs to Him. God has the power to take it all if He chooses. Keeping this knowledge in the back of our minds will produce a generous attitude.

Grace giving releases pressure. If believers give in a systematic manner, they will put aside each time that which they have determined to give, and then there will be no pressure. One may use the Old Testament pattern of ten percent if they feel more comfortable with that. It may very well be more than ten percent, but it should be done consistently and not grudgingly.

Grace giving releases covetousness. There will never be the nagging temptation of what one could have done with the money if it had been kept.

Grace giving promotes cheerfulness. When we put aside the portion that belongs to the Lord, we can give with a cheerful attitude.

Grace giving promotes worship. Giving is an act of worship, or worth-ship! To the extent that we appreciate God's Word, His church, and His person, we will give.

God's work done God's way will never suffer for God's abundant provision.

CHAPTER 11

A GLIMPSE OF THE CHRISTIAN'S ACCOUNTABILITY

We need to catch a small glimpse of two areas of the Christian's personal accountability before God: personal sin and personal stewardship.

Christians are not sinless people! The Bible does not hide this fact. Noah was a sinner. Abraham was a sinner. Isaac was a sinner. It appeared that Jacob's life was filled with deceit. David was a sinner. Paul said that in his flesh dwelt no good thing (Rom. 7:15-20). Peter actually denied His Lord three times (Matt. 26:69-75).

When Jesus came to earth, He went to where the sinners were. He hung out with the likes of despised tax collectors, prostitutes, fishermen, lepers, and the common people. He did not go to the religious crowd.

The Bible never sugarcoats the lives of God's chosen. God paints us with warts and all! As we have seen, our sin nature is tied to our physical body (Rom. 7:18). It doesn't take a theologian to understand that as long as we remain connected to this body we will retain both the temptation and capacity to sin. As the songwriter so eloquently said, "Prone to wander, Lord I feel it; prone to leave the God I love."

Our flesh continuously wars against the Holy Spirit and the Spirit against the flesh. This provides a constant source of inner conflict (Gal. 5:17). Until death or the rapture, this conflict will go on.

SIN'S CONSEQUENCES

The mature believer is consciously aware that the potential to sin is ever present. Along with that knowledge is the awareness that sin always has its consequences. Personal sin results in the discipline of God. Even though we are saved forever by God's amazing grace, God is a holy God, and He must remain holy. In order to do so, He must always adjust that which is not right to His absolute righteous standard. His righteousness demands it. God does not turn a blind eye to our personal sin. When we are born again into God's forever family it means that God is our heavenly father. We have a Father-son relationship (Gal. 3:26). God deals with us as His children.

> And you have forgotten the exhortation which speaks to you as to sons: "My son, do not despise the chastening of the LORD, nor be discouraged when you are rebuked by Him; For whom the LORD loves He chastens, and scourges every son whom He receives." If you endure chastening, God deals with you as with sons; for what son is there whom a father does not chasten? But if you are without chastening, of which all have become partakers, then you are illegitimate and not sons. Furthermore, we have had human fathers who corrected us, and we paid them respect. Shall we not much more readily be in subjection to the Father of spirits and live? For they indeed for a few days chastened us as seemed best to them, but He for our profit, that we may be partakers of His holiness. Now no chastening seems to be joyful for the present, but painful; nevertheless, afterward it yields the peaceable fruit of righteousness to those who have been trained by it. (Heb. 12:5-11)

Every good father disciplines his children. God is the best Father of all! He disciplines all who belong to Him. In fact, His discipline is positive proof that we belong to Him. If God does not discipline us for our sin, then we really do not belong to Him.

His chastening at times is not joyful but painful, but it always yields the peaceable fruit of righteousness. Remember, this word *righteousness* is "dikaiosune." It means that God's discipline always fits the crime and balances the scales perfectly. God's discipline is never too much or too little. When discipline occurs, the issue is settled, and peace is restored.

When my children were small, I might ask them to do a small chore around the house. If they disobeyed me and failed to do as I asked, there would be discipline. The anxiety for them was always in the waiting. They wanted most often to get it over with. Once the discipline had been carried out it yielded the peaceable fruit of righteousness. The issue was settled, and peace was restored. It is the same with our Father in heaven.

God told Israel to go in and take the Promised Land. The people were ready to comply. They knew that it would mean they would have to fight for it, but they were ready. They told Moses what they planned to do once the land was theirs. They would build sheepfolds for their livestock and cities for their children. With this in mind they were ready to arm themselves and march out. They said they would not return until every one of them had received the inheritance that was theirs.

Moses said that what they had in mind was commendable. If they would do this, God would drive out their enemies. They would then return blameless before the Lord. But what would happen if they did not follow through?

> But if you do not do so, then take note, you have sinned against the Lord; and be sure your sin will find you out. (Num. 32:23)

Note the phrase, "Be sure your sin will find you out." We must take this warning into account. It is never possible to hide our sin from God. King David wrote:

> Where can I go from Your Spirit? Or where can I flee from Your presence? If I ascend into heaven, You are there; If I make my bed in hell, behold, You are there. If I take the wings of the morning, and dwell in the uttermost parts of the sea, even there Your hand shall lead me, and Your right hand shall hold me. If I say, "Surely the darkness shall fall on me," Even the night shall be light about me; Indeed, the darkness shall not hide from You, but the night shines as the day; The darkness and the light are both alike to You. (Ps. 139:7-12)

David said that we can run from God, but we cannot hide. We can run up as high as the sky itself or down as low as the earth. We can go right or left, but we can never get away from God. We can run into the darkness, but God can see in the dark. The great hound of heaven will find us.

THE SIN OF ACHAN

One illustration is worth a thousand words. There is a graphic testimony of one who attempted to hide sin from God. God uses his example to teach us that we cannot cover our sin and that sin always has consequences.

God was moving Israel into the land that He had promised them. Under the leadership of Joshua, Israel began to destroy the Canaanites. When the Jews came to Jericho God miraculously gave Jericho into their hands. Rahab's life and the lives of her family were spared because she had hidden Israel's spies. God told the Jews that all the gold and silver and bronze and iron were to be placed into the tabernacle (Josh. 6:24). But note these words:

> But the children of Israel committed a trespass regarding
> the accursed things, for Achan the son of Carmi, the son
> of Zabdi, the son of Zerah, of the tribe of Judah, took of the
> accursed things; so the anger of the LORD burned against
> the children of Israel. (Josh. 7:1)

This was one of those quiet secret sins that seemingly no one knew about or certainly wouldn't care about. It was just a small thing according to our standards today but not according to God. His character is perfect. He must always judge sin. His integrity cannot be compromised. God had said, "Be sure your sin will find you out." Though no one in Israel was aware of Achan's sin, the omniscient God was.

> O LORD, You have searched me and known me. You know
> my sitting down and my rising up You understand my
> thought afar off. You comprehend my path and my lying
> down, and are acquainted with all my ways. For there is
> not a word on my tongue, but behold, O LORD, You know
> it altogether. You have hedged me behind and before and
> laid Your hand upon me. Such knowledge is too wonderful
> for me; It is high, I cannot attain it. (Ps. 139:1-6)

God knows our thoughts before we think them, our words before we speak them, and our ways before we do them. Because of Achan's sin, the anger of the Lord burned against the children of Israel (Josh. 7:1). As a consequence, Israel began to lose battles. They went against Ai thinking that God would continue to give them victories over their enemies. But not so. The men of Ai defeated the Jews, who were under God's discipline. Joshua was confused; he began to whine and complain. God's response was quick and decisive.

> So the LORD said to Joshua: "Get up! Why do you lie
> thus on your face? Israel has sinned, and they have also
> transgressed My covenant which I commanded them. For
> they have even taken some of the accursed things, and

146

have both stolen and deceived; and they have also put it among their own stuff." (Josh. 7:10-11)

We might rationalize today, "But God, is that so horrible a sin? It is just a small thing when placed against what was happening there!"

Someone has written about the war that was lost for the lack of a horseshoe nail. The commander led the troops into battle. A horseshoe nail came loose and his horse lost the shoe, stumbled, and fell. The commander was thrown to the ground. The commander was lost and the men did not follow through on the charge and because of this the battle was lost. The battle was the most important in the war, and because the battle was lost, the war was lost. Thus the war was lost all because of a tiny horseshoe nail. No sin is ever small to a holy God.

God told Joshua to find the forbidden spoils of war in their midst because they could not realize success in battle until it was removed. God told Joshua to search the families one by one until it was found. Joshua began to confront the each family.

> Then he brought his household man by man, and Achan the son of Carmi, the son of Zabdi, the son of Zerah, of the tribe of Judah, was taken. Now Joshua said to Achan, "My son, I beg you, give glory to the LORD God of Israel, and make confession to Him, and tell me now what you have done; do not hide it from me." And Achan answered Joshua and said, "Indeed I have sinned against the LORD God of Israel, and this is what I have done: When I saw among the spoils a beautiful Babylonian garment, two hundred shekels of silver, and a wedge of gold weighing fifty shekels, I coveted them and took them. And there they are, hidden in the earth in the midst of my tent, with the silver under it." (Josh. 7:18-20)

Achan was guilty, and he confessed, but sin always has its consequences. Achan and his entire family were killed. This seems to be severe punishment for the crime. With God, the judgment always fits the crime.

What the testimony of Achan is designed to show is that God is a holy God and He will not tolerate sin. We cannot hide our sin from God.

> He who covers his sins will not prosper, but whoever confesses and forsakes them will have mercy. (Prov. 28:13)

THE SIN OF DAVID

As a young man, David had a heart for God, so much so that God selected this simple shepherd boy to be the king of all Israel. His family produced the line from which the Messiah would come. His throne is the throne upon which our Lord will one day reign. Yet David became a tremendous example of how believers can and do sin and how God disciplines those whom He loves. David sinned against God.

There came a time in Israel's history when all the soldiers went off to war, but David, the warrior king, stayed home. One morning he got up early and walked out on his roof and looked across the way and saw a woman bathing. She was very beautiful. David was overcome with lust. He found out that her name was Bathsheba and that she was the wife of Uriah the Hittite.

David had the woman brought to him, and he took her. She bowed before his wishes because he was the king. When she informed him later that she was pregnant with his child, David sent to the battlefield for Uriah. David hoped that her husband would go in to his wife so that Uriah would think that the child was his. Uriah refused, saying that he would not enjoy his home life while his men were fighting.

David was frantic. He had Uriah shipped to the front line of battle where he was killed. David tried everything to cover his sin, but the Bible says, "This thing which David did displeased the LORD" (2 Sam. 11:27).

God sent Nathan the prophet to visit David. Nathan gave David an illustration. He said, "Your majesty, there was this very wealthy man who had thousands of sheep, but this neighbor had one little lamb that had grown up with his children. And a guest came to eat with the rich man and the rich man stole the little lamb from the poor man in order to feed his guest."

David was angry and lashed out. How dare that man do that! "That man shall die and repay fourfold for the lamb that was taken because he had no pity" (2 Sam. 12:6).

Then there was a long silence. Nathan said simply, "You are the man" (2 Sam. 12:7). David's sin had found him out. It always does. David's confession was, "I have sinned against the LORD."

CONFESSION OF SIN

The guilt eventually caused David to confess his sin. This is the key to restored fellowship with God. The conviction led to David's confession. It is recorded for us in Psalm 51.

> Have mercy upon me, O God, according to Your lovingkindness; according to the multitude of Your tender mercies, blot out my transgressions. Wash me thoroughly from my iniquity, and cleanse me from my sin. For I acknowledge my transgressions, and my sin is always before me. Against You, You only, have I sinned, and done this evil in Your sight. (Ps. 51:1-4).

David's confession began with God. Did he not sin against Bathsheba? Yes. Did he not sin against Uriah? Yes. Did he not sin against the entire nation of Israel as its king? Yes. David realized, however, that his sin was ultimately against God. He had rebelled against Him, and that led to the domino affect that touched all the other lives.

> That You may be found just when You speak, and blameless when You judge. Behold, I was brought forth in iniquity,

149

and in sin my mother conceived me. Behold, You desire truth in the inward parts and in the hidden part You will make me to know wisdom. Purge me with hyssop, and I shall be clean; Wash me, and I shall be whiter than snow. Make me hear joy and gladness, that the bones You have broken may rejoice. Hide Your face from my sins, and blot out all my iniquities. Create in me a clean heart, O God, and renew a steadfast spirit within me. Do not cast me away from Your presence, and do not take Your Holy Spirit from me. Restore to me the joy of Your salvation, and uphold me by Your generous Spirit. Then I will teach transgressors Your ways, and sinners shall be converted to You. Deliver me from the guilt of bloodshed, O God, the God of my salvation, and my tongue shall sing aloud of Your righteousness. (Ps. 51:4b-14)

David cast himself entirely upon God's grace. There was no arrogance and no prideful attitude. He did not blame others. He took full responsibility. He brought out all the details. He cried out to God for forgiveness.

FORGIVENESS OF SIN

David's greatest desire was for God to restore to him the joy of his salvation. David had not lost his relationship with God but his personal fellowship. Following his confession, he was forgiven. Forgiven! That is one of the sweetest words in any language. David's joy returned.

Blessed is he whose transgression is forgiven, whose sin is covered. Blessed is the man to whom the LORD does not impute iniquity and in whose spirit there is no deceit. (Ps. 32:1-2)

I acknowledged my sin to You, and my iniquity I have not hidden. I said, "I will confess my transgressions to the LORD," and You forgave the iniquity of my sin. (Ps. 32:5-6)

David pleaded with God not to remove His Spirit from him. In the Old Testament God sent His Spirit upon certain people for a particular purpose, but when that purpose had been accomplished, God's Spirit departed. This is not the case with us today. God's Spirit is forever with us because He is forever in us. He will never leave us for any reason. He remains the guarantee that we belong to Jesus Christ (Eph. 1:13-14).

David never forgot that he was still a sinner, but he was a sinner with a passion to tell other people about the living God (Ps. 51:13).

CONSEQUENCES OF SIN

Confession removes the guilt of sin, but it does not remove sin's consequences. David had to endure God's discipline for his sin. His penalties were not as severe as they were for Achan, but God knows what is needed.

> "I gave you your master's house and your master's wives into your keeping, and gave you the house of Israel and Judah. And if that had been too little, I also would have given you much more! Why have you despised the commandment of the LORD, to do evil in His sight? You have killed Uriah the Hittite with the sword; you have taken his wife to be your wife, and have killed him with the sword of the people of Ammon. Now therefore, the sword shall never depart from your house, because you have despised Me, and have taken the wife of Uriah the Hittite to be your wife." Thus says the LORD: "Behold, I will raise up adversity against you from your own house; and I will take your wives before your eyes and give them to your neighbor, and he shall lie with your wives in the sight of this sun. For you did it secretly, but I will do this thing before all Israel, before the sun." (2 Sam. 12:7-12)

As a consequence for his sin, God took peace from David's home. David's son became his enemy. David's wives left him and went to his neighbor openly and publicly. David's enemies mocked the God of Israel, and David's child died. Sin always has its consequences.

PERSONAL ACCOUNTABILITY

We are responsible to God as His children to live our lives pleasing to Him. Our challenge is to allow the Spirit of God to glorify Christ through us. The way to do this is to keep short sin accounts with God. However, we do not always cooperate with the Spirit. We either grieve Him by consciously doing that which displeases Him (Eph. 4:25-32), or we quench Him by not allowing Him to lead us (1 Thess. 5:19). Both will result in God's discipline.

Always remember that God's discipline is proof positive that we belong to Him and that He loves us. When the Holy Spirit convicts us of sin, we can adjust ourselves to God's righteous standard by judging ourselves.

> For if we would judge ourselves, we would not be judged.
> (1 Cor. 11:31)

When we judge ourselves, we deal with our personal sins before God. We judge ourselves by personally and privately acknowledging our sin to God.

> If we confess our sins, He is faithful and just to forgive
> us our sins and to cleanse us from all unrighteousness. (1
> Jn. 1:9)

Confession is not some public religious display. The word *confess* means "to agree." The moment that the Holy Spirit convicts us of a wrong thought, word, or deed, we are to agree. The moment that we confess, God forgives. This judgment occurs within the solitude of our minds before God alone. This is our privilege because we are "believer priests" (Rev. 1:6; 5:10; 1 Pet. 2:5, 9). When we ignore the convicting work of the Spirit and fail to agree with Him, we grieve Him. When He is grieved, God must discipline us.

> But when we are judged, we are chastened by the Lord, that
> we may not be condemned with the world. (1 Cor. 11:32)

God's chastening is for Christians only. His disciplining hand on believers sets us apart from unbelievers.

THE JUDGMENT SEAT OF CHRIST

Another area of personal accountability before God concerns our works. Again, the Bible makes it quite clear that we are not declared right before God by our good deeds (Titus 3:5). However, we have learned that God has uniquely gifted every Christian to perform a stewardship responsibility in order to build up the body of Christ. We have not been gifted the same nor given the same responsibilities, but we all have one thing in common. God will one day judge each of us for our effort and spiritual productivity.

> But why do you judge your brother? Or why do you show
> contempt for your brother? For we shall all stand before
> the judgment seat of Christ. For it is written: "As I live
> says the LORD, Every knee shall bow to Me. And every
> tongue shall confess to God." So then each of us shall give
> account of himself to God. (Rom. 14:10-12)

Judgment seat in the Greek is the word "bema." The bema, or rewarding stand of judges, was established to reward those competing in the sporting games of the ancient world. Our righteous judge will one day reward believers for their work. Paul clearly connects the reason for this judgment with the particular grace stewardship given to believers.

> Who then is Paul, and who is Apollos, but ministers through whom you believed, as the Lord gave to each one? I planted, Apollos watered, but God gave the increase. So then neither he who plants is anything, nor he who waters, but God who gives the increase. Now he who plants and he who waters are one, and each one will receive his own reward according to his own labor. For we are God's fellow workers; you are God's field, you are God's building. According to the grace of God which was given to me, as a wise master builder I have laid the foundation, and another builds on it. But let each one take heed how he builds on it. For no other foundation can anyone lay than that which is laid, which is Jesus Christ. Now if anyone builds on this foundation with gold, silver, precious stones, wood, hay, straw, each one's work will become clear; for the Day will declare it, because it will be revealed by fire; and the fire will test each one's work, of what sort it is. If anyone's work which he has built on it endures, he will receive a reward. If anyone's work is burned, he will suffer loss; but he himself will be saved, yet so as through fire. (1 Cor. 3:5-15)

Paul referred to the Corinthians as babes in Christ. He said that he had fed them with the milk of the word because they were not capable of understanding the deeper truths. He used their division over following men rather than Christ as proof of this. Paul then explained that all of these men were ministers through whom they had believed the gospel. All of these men had a part to play in building the body of Christ. They were to work together as a team.

This provokes an interesting question. Since the servants work on the same team, and since God is the one producing the ministry, does the quality of our work make any difference at all? Yes. Note these words: each one will receive his own reward according to his own labor. That is as it should be. Why? Paul said the body grows by that which every joint supplies (Eph. 4:16).

Paul used three metaphors to help us understand his point.

- *We are God's fellow workers.* Paul was speaking of the apostles. The apostles work was not their own. Corinth was God's church, not Paul's or Apollos's or Peter's. They were to work together for the building of the church.

- *You are God's field.* The church here is pictured like God's cultivated field. These people were familiar with agriculture. There must be preparation of the soil, the planting of the seed, the fertilizing, the watering, the weeding, and then the harvesting. That is what ministry is all about! Some need the seed of the gospel to be planted in their minds, some need to be taught, some need encouragement, some need to be challenged, some need to be disciplined, and some need to be culled out.

- *You are God's building.* The Corinthian church also understood how a building was put together. Some are just beginning to lay a foundation in the scripture and are in need of the milk of the word; some have the walls already built and they are sturdy and need deeper teaching; some are ready for the roof to be placed, they are mature and in need of meat. First you have those who lay the foundation then the framers, then the construction crew, then the bricklayers, the sheetrock, and the painters.

Paul applied these metaphors to the church. He had laid the foundation but another built on that foundation. He had preached the gospel, but Apollos came along and confirmed what Paul had taught. He may have picked some fruit from the seeds that Paul had planted.

From the Day of Pentecost to this very day, the framers and the construction crew have come along to build upon the foundation laid by the apostles and prophets. God has equipped every believer of every generation to do some building. Observe carefully the warning: but let each one take heed how he builds on it. *Take heed* means to be very sensitive about something. Do not take this responsibility lightly.

This introduces a quality aspect into this building process. We are to use the gifts that God has given to us wisely. As one of my seminary professors used to say, "We are not to build a chicken coop on a foundation built for a skyscraper." The church is being built upon the identity of Jesus Christ as the God-Man (Matt. 16:13).

The judgment seat of Christ has everything to do with our giftedness. All believers are going to do some building, but the quality of what is built is the issue.

Six building materials are mentioned: gold, silver, precious stone, wood, hay, and stubble. These materials vary in the degree of value from gold being the most valuable down to stubble, which has almost no value at all. We conclude from this that God takes note of the quality of work that each believer is doing.

Another obvious difference in the building materials is that one category is combustible and the other is not. Gold, silver, and precious stone will not burn; but wood, hay, and stubble will burn. This gives us the impression that fire is going to be involved in the judgment process. Remember that fire in the Bible is associated with God's judgment. Fire is used to purify, to purge.

The result of the fire is that each one's work will become clear. Each believer's work will be brought into sharp focus. The fire of God's judgment will burn through our works and that which is left becomes the basis for our reward.

God has set aside a special time that will be used for the purpose of judging the believers works. That judgment day is called the judgment seat of Christ.

> For we must all appear before the judgment seat of Christ that each one may receive the things done in the body, according to what he has done, whether good or bad. (2 Cor. 5:10)

Either we are making wise investments of our spiritual gifts and our time within the body of Christ, or we are not. God will bring our works to light and expose them to His judgment.

The individual work of every single child of God is going to be judged and rewarded according to its quality, not its quantity. Every believer's work will be passed through the fire. The quality of the work is not revealed in this life, but it will be revealed at a special time and place when the Lord returns. One who knows all the facts will judge it. That's why we are specifically told not to judge or evaluate any believer prior to the coming of Christ. If the work passes through the fire without being consumed, that believer will receive a reward.

There are various crowns named in scripture as rewards awaiting faithful believers:

- **Crown of Joy**–given to believers who share the gospel
  For what is our hope, or joy, or crown of rejoicing? Is it not even you in the presence of our Lord Jesus Christ at His coming? For you are our glory and joy. (1 Thess. 2:19)

- **Crown of Righteousness**–given to believers who have kept the faith in anticipation of the appearing of Jesus Christ
  I have fought the good fight, I have finished the race, I have kept the faith. Finally, there is laid up for me the crown of righteousness, which the Lord, the righteous Judge, will give to me on that Day, and not to me only but also to all who have loved His appearing. (2 Tim. 4:7-8)

- **Crown of Life**–given to believers who persevere through the trials of life
  Blessed is the man who endures temptation; for when he has been approved, he will receive the crown of life which the Lord has promised to those who love Him. (Jas. 1:12)

- **Crown of Glory**–given to pastors who faithfully feed and meet the spiritual needs of the church
  The elders who are among you I exhort, I who am a fellow elder and a witness of the sufferings of Christ, and also a partaker of the glory that will be revealed: Shepherd the

flock of God which is among you, serving as overseers, not by compulsion but willingly, not for dishonest gain but eagerly; nor as being lords over those entrusted to you, but being examples to the flock; and when the Chief Shepherd appears, you will receive the crown of glory that does not fade away. (1 Pet. 5:1-4)

DO BUSINESS UNTIL I COME

Jesus was approaching Jerusalem after passing through Jericho. The people thought that the kingdom was going to immediately appear. This was not going to be the case, so Jesus gave this parable. A certain nobleman (speaking of Christ) went to a far country to receive for himself a kingdom. This speaks of the fact that Jesus was going to die and be resurrected from the dead and ascend back into heaven with the promise to return and establish His kingdom.

He called ten of his servants and gave each of them ten minas. A mina was approximately a three month's wage, so it was a lot of money. The nobleman told the servants to wisely invest the money while he was away. He commanded, "Do business until I come." The citizens, however, sent a delegation and told the nobleman that they did not want him to rule over them.

The application is clear. We are servants of Jesus Christ. The King is away and we are to be busy doing His business until He returns. He has equipped us to serve His church. We must spend these gifts well. We are to work hard to carry out our stewardship responsibility. We are to produce good fruit for His glory. He is coming back, and we will be judged for how we have spent our lives (2 Cor. 5:10).

Finally the nobleman returned. Upon his arrival the servants came before him one by one. The first servant reported that he had wisely invested the nobleman's money and had a good return. His minas had earned ten more. The reward for him was to rule over ten cities.

The second servant also made a good investment but not as much as the first. His minas made five minas. Again the reward was equal to the investment. He was given rule over five cities. Still the nobleman was pleased.

The third servant, however, had not done well. He said to the nobleman that he knew that the master was a strict or stern man. He collected what he did not deposit and reaped what he did not sow. The nobleman saw that as an excuse for failure. He really didn't think the master was going to return. The nobleman took the money from the lazy servant and gave it to the others. However, the unprofitable servant did not lose his life, because he was still a servant. The nobleman then told the servants to bring all of those who did not want him to rule and kill them.

Our King will someday return as He promised. We must spend our lives and giftedness well. We will be judged for what we do. Judgment day is coming.

> Walk in a manner worthy of the Lord, to please Him in all respects, bearing fruit in every good work and increasing in the knowledge of God; strengthened with all power, according to His glorious might, for the attaining of all steadfastness and patience. (Col. 1:10-11)

Christians are connected to Christ by birth, by position, and by possession. The Holy Spirit regenerates us by God's living Word, the gospel, and baptizes us into the body of Christ. We become new creations in Christ. God's Spirit also lives within our bodies making them temples of the living God. We are forever sealed in Christ by the Spirit of God, equipped by the Spirit and taught by the Spirit. It is the responsibility of each believer to allow the Holy Spirit to magnify Jesus Christ through us to the world. It is my sincere prayer that this book has accomplished its purpose, revealing to us precious glimpses of God's magnificent grace.

APPENDIX
SCRIPTURE MEMORIZATION

Suggestions for beginning a memorization program:

- Write each verse on a 3 X 5 card. Write the scripture reference on the back. Use the cards like flash cards. Try looking at the reference and quoting the verse or looking at the verse and quoting where it is found.
- Put a red mark in your Bible beside each verse on this list so that when you are studying the Bible, you will pay particular attention to the verse in its context and recognize it as one of your memory verses.
- Set a goal of memorizing one verse a week for the first month, then increase to two verses per week, and continue to progress to a level that is comfortable for you. Work at your own pace.
- Set up a partner system. Practice with your spouse in the car, or call a friend on a weekly basis. It is important to be accountable to someone.
- Always review. Review often the verses that you have already committed to memory.

MEMORY VERSES FOR BEGINNERS

SALVATION:

Ephesians 2:8-9	2 Corinthians 5:21	John 3:16-18	John 1:12-14
Romans 3:10,23	Romans 4:4,5	Romans 6:23	Acts 16:31

| Galatians 2:16 | James 2:10 | John 10:28 | 1 John 5:11-13 |
| Acts 13:38-39 | | | |

CHRISTIAN LIFE:

Hebrews 12:6	1 John 1:9	Romans 12:1-2	1 Timothy 4:12
1 Cor. 11:31-32	Proverbs 3:5-6	1 Cor. 10:13	1 Peter 2:2
Psalm 37:4,5	Eph. 4:30	Ephesians 5:18	1 Samuel 12:24
Hebrews 12:1-2	1 Cor. 15:58	1 Thess. 5:19	Galatians 5:16-17
John 15:5	Romans 8:28-30		

MEMORY VERSES FOR ADVANCED

These verses help the student think his or her way through the subject matter of the book. When learned in this order and placed together, they can help you to think your way through the Bible.

Romans 1:16-17	Rom. 2:11, 14-15	Romans 3:10	Romans 3:19-20
Romans 3:21-25	Romans 5:1,6,8	Romans 5:12	Romans 5:20
Romans 6:1-3	Romans 7:7-14	Romans 7:18	Romans 8:1-4
Romans 8:14-16	Romans 8:32	Romans 8:38-39	Romans 9:18
Romans 10:9-10	Romans 10:13	Romans 10:17	Romans 11:6
Romans 11:33	Romans 12:3	Romans 13:1	Romans 13:11
Romans 14:8	Romans 14:10	Romans 15:1	1 Cor. 1:18
1 Cor. 2:2	1 Cor. 2:9-10	1 Cor. 2:14	1 Cor. 3:11
1 Cor. 4:2	1 Cor. 6:12	1 Cor. 6:19-20	1 Cor. 9:16-17
1 Cor. 9:19	1 Cor. 10:13	1 Cor. 10:31	1 Cor. 12:11
1 Cor. 13:4-8	1 Cor. 14:33a	1 Cor. 15:20-22	2 Cor. 4:3-4
2 Cor. 4:16-18	2 Cor. 5:10	2 Cor. 5:17	2 Cor. 12:9
Galatians 1:8-9	Galatians 2:20	Galatians 3:10-13	Galatians 3:19
Galatians 3:26	Galatians 5:1	Galatians 5:16-17	Galatians 5:22-23
Galatians 6:2	Galatians 6:7	Ephesians 1:13-14	Ephesians 2:10
Ephesians 3:20-21	Ephesians 4:11	Ephesians 4:29-30	Ephesians 5:15-16
Ephesians 6:1-4	Ephesians 6:11	Philippians 1:21	Philippians 2:5-8
Philippians 3:7	Philippians 3:9-10	Phil. 3:20-21	Philippians 4:4
Philippians 4:6	Philippians 4:13	Philippians 4:19	Colossians 2:6
Colossians 2:13-14	Colossians 3:2	Colossians 3:23	Colossians 4:6
1 Thess. 2:4	1 Thess. 4:16-17	1 Thess. 5:9	1 Thess. 5:14
2 Thess. 2:13-14	2 Timothy 2:15	2 Timothy 3:16-17	Titus 3:5

Titus 3:8	Hebrews 4:12	Hebrews 4:15	Hebrews 7:9
Hebrews 11:1	Hebrews 11:6	Hebrews 13:5-8	James 1:2-6
James 1:8	James 1:17-19	James 1:22	James 4:10
James 4:17	James 5:20	1 Peter 2:24	1 Peter 3:10
1 Peter 3:15	1 Peter 3:18	1 Peter 5:6-7	1 John 1:5
1 John 1:7-8	1 John 4:8	1 John 4:10-11	1 John 5:20
Revelation 3:20	Revelation 14:11	Matthew 6:21	Matthew 6:33
Matthew 7:7	Matthew 7:12	Matthew 11:28-30	Matthew 12:31
Matthew 12:34	Matthew 15:19	Matthew 19:26	Matthew 21:22
Matthew 22:37-40	Matthew 28:6	Matthew 28:19-20	Mark 10:45
Mark 11:24	Mark 16:15	Luke 1:37	Luke 14:26
Luke 16:13	Luke 19:10	John 1:1-3	John 1:18
John 3:3	John 3:36	John 4:24	John 5:5
John 5:24	John 6:37	John 6:39	John 6:47
John 8:32	John 8:58	John 10:10	John 11:35
John 12:24	John 14:1-4	John 14:6	John 15:8
John 16:7-11	John 16:33	John 20:30-31	Acts 1:8
Acts 4:12	Acts 5:29	Acts 5:41-42	Acts 8:35
Acts 10:34	Acts 13:38-29	Acts 13:48	Acts 14:16-17
Acts 17:31	Acts 20:24	Genesis 2:15-17	Genesis 3:15
Genesis 15:6	Exodus 3:14	Leviticus 17:11	Deut. 6:4-9
Deut. 21:22-23	Joshua 24:24	Psalm 2:12	Psalm 14:1
Psalm 19:1	Psalm 23:1-6	Psalm 24:1	Psalm 27:1
Psalm 32:1-2	Psalm 51:5	Psalm 90:2	Psalm 119:9-16
Psalm 139:1-12	Proverbs 3:1-6	Ecclesiastes 7:20	Isaiah 7:14
Isaiah 53:6	Isaiah 55:11	Isaiah 64:6	Jeremiah 17:9
Daniel 4:34-35	Zechariah 12:10		

Scripture Index

Matt. 28:19	134	Rom. 5:5	55
Jn. 1:12	42	Rom. 5:12	6
Jn. 3:2	7	Rom. 6:3	95
Jn. 3:3	7	Rom. 7:1	91
Jn. 3:4	7	Rom. 7:2-3	94
Jn. 3:7	7	Rom. 7:4	94
Jn. 3:31	37	Rom. 7:4b	95
Jn. 6:63	11	Rom. 7:7-11	35
Jn. 8:44	41	Rom. 7:18	31
Jn. 8:47a	18	Rom. 8:9	56
Jn. 10:27-30	79	Rom. 8:16	42
Jn. 14:1-3	76	Rom. 8:23-25	76
Jn. 14:16-20	19	Rom. 8:29	38
Jn. 14:23-24	97	Rom. 8:31	79
Jn. 15:3	8	Rom. 8:32	80
Jn. 16:12-15	122	Rom. 8:33	80
Acts 1:4b-5	26	Rom. 8:35-37	81
Acts 2:1-12	27	Rom. 8:38-39	82
Acts 2:1-4	55	Rom. 10:17	86
Acts 2:42	132	Rom. 14:10-12	153
Acts 8:1	57	1 Cor. 1:2	29
Acts 8:3	57	1 Cor. 1:4	110
Acts 9:4	57	1 Cor. 1:14-17	8
Acts 9:31	58	1 Cor. 1:17	122
Acts 11:15-16	28	1 Cor. 1:18	123
Acts 11:22	58	1 Cor. 1:19	123
Acts 11:26	1, 58	1 Cor. 1:20	124
Acts 12:1	58	1 Cor. 1:26-31	125
Acts 12:5	58	1 Cor. 1:30	29
Acts 14:17	4	1 Cor. 2:6	161
Acts 17:30-31	37	1 Cor. 2:7-9	127
Acts 26:18	42	1 Cor. 2:10	127
Acts 26:28	2	1 Cor. 2:11-13	128
Acts 7:48-50	52	1 Cor. 3:2	120
Rom. 1:16	12	1 Cor. 3:5-15	154
Rom. 3:23	33	1 Cor. 6:19-20	55

ENDNOTES

1. Roy B. Zuck, *The Speaker's Quote Book* (Grand Rapids: Kregel Publications, 1997), 33.
2. Botanical Record Breakers, guardian.co.uk, June 12, 2008.
3. Zuck, 34.
4. R. B. Thieme, Tape Series: *Romans* (Houston: Barachah, 1966).
5. Howard G. Hendricks, classroom quote, Dallas Theological Seminary, 1980.
6. S. Lewis Johnson, Tape series: *Romans* (Dallas: Believers Chapel, 1990)
7. Edwin Blum, *The Bible Knowledge Commentary: New Testament*, "Romans" (SP Publications, Inc., 1983)
8. M. R. DeHann. *Galatians* (Grand Rapids: Zondervan Publishing House), 67.
9. Ibid, p. 68.
10. John MacArthur. *MacArthur's New Testament Commentary: Hebrews.* (Chicago: Moody Bible Institute, 1983, electronic)
11. Duane A. Litfin. *The Bible Knowledge Commentary: New Testament,* "1 Timothy" (Hiawatha, Iowa: Parsons Technology, 1983).
12. John MacArthur. MacArthur's New Testament Commentary: 2 Timothy (Chicago: Moody Bible Institute, 1995, electronic)
13. MacArthur
14. Arnold G. Fruchtenbaum. Online Studies, Study Code, MBS149 (Ariel Ministries)

CPSIA information can be obtained at www.ICGtesting.com
Printed in the USA
LVOW06s1153060614

388812LV00001B/95/P